U.S.-China Relations:

An Affirmative Agenda,

A Responsible Course

U.S.-China Relations:

An Affirmative Agenda,

A Responsible Course

Report of an
Independent Task Force

Sponsored by the Council on Foreign Relations

Founded in 1921, the Council on Foreign Relations is an independent, national membership organization and a nonpartisan center for scholars dedicated to producing and disseminating ideas so that individual and corporate members, as well as policymakers, journalists, students, and interested citizens in the United States and other countries, can better understand the world and the foreign policy choices facing the United States and other governments. The Council does this by convening meetings; conducting a wide-ranging Studies program; publishing *Foreign Affairs*, the preeminent journal covering international affairs and U.S. foreign policy; maintaining a diverse membership; sponsoring Independent Task Forces; and providing up-to-date information about the world and U.S. foreign policy on the Council's website, CFR.org.

THE COUNCIL TAKES NO INSTITUTIONAL POSITION ON POLICY ISSUES AND HAS NO AFFILIATION WITH THE U.S. GOVERNMENT. ALL STATEMENTS OF FACT AND EXPRESSIONS OF OPINION CONTAINED IN ITS PUBLICATIONS ARE THE SOLE RESPONSIBILITY OF THE AUTHOR OR AUTHORS.

The Council will sponsor an Independent Task Force when (1) an issue of current and critical importance to U.S. foreign policy arises, and (2) it seems that a group diverse in backgrounds and perspectives may, nonetheless, be able to reach a meaningful consensus on a policy through private and nonpartisan deliberations. Typically, a Task Force meets between two and five times over a brief period to ensure the relevance of its work.

Upon reaching a conclusion, an Independent Task Force issues a report, and the Council publishes its text and posts it on the Council website, CFR.org. Task Force reports reflect a strong and meaningful policy consensus, with Task Force members endorsing the general policy thrust and judgments reached by the group, though not necessarily every finding and recommendation. Task Force members who join the consensus may submit additional or dissenting views, which are included in the final report. "Chairman's Reports" are signed by Task Force chairs only and are usually preceded or followed by full Task Force reports. Upon reaching a conclusion, a Task Force may also ask individuals who were not members of the Task Force to associate themselves with the Task Force report to enhance its impact. All Task Force reports "benchmark" their findings against current administration policy to make explicit areas of agreement and disagreement. The Task Force is solely responsible for its report. The Council takes no institutional position.

For further information about the Council or this Independent Task Force, please write to Publications, Council on Foreign Relations, 58 East 68th Street, New York, NY 10021, or call the Communications office at 212-434-9888. Visit our website, CFR.org.

Task Force Chairs

Dennis C. Blair

Dennis C. Blair

Carla A. Hills

Carla A. Hills

Project Director

Frank Jannuzi

Frank Sampson Jannuzi

Task Force Members

Roger C. Altman

Peter E. Bass

Dennis C. Blair

Harold Brown*

Ashton B. Carter

Charles W. Freeman III

Aaron L. Friedberg*

Paul Gewirtz

Maurice R. Greenberg*

Harry Harding*

Carla A. Hills

Frank Sampson Jannuzi

Michael H. Jordan

Virginia Ann Kamsky*

David M. Lampton

Nicholas R. Lardy

Herbert Levin*

Cheng Li

Winston Lord*

Xiaobo Lu

Evan S. Medeiros

James C. Mulvenon

Andrew J. Nathan

Stephen A. Orlins

Evans J.R. Revere

Bradley H. Roberts

Alan D. Romberg

Randy Schriver*

Wendy R. Sherman

Arthur Waldron*

*The individual has endorsed the report and submitted an additional or a dissenting view.

Contents

Foreword

No relationship will be as important to the twenty-first century as the one between the United States, the world's great power, and China, the world's rising power. China's development is directly transforming the lives of one-fifth of the world's population and is otherwise influencing billions more. China's rapid economic growth, expanding regional and global influence, continued military modernization, and lagging political reform are also shifting the geopolitical terrain and contributing to uncertainty about China's future course. After thirty-five years of "engagement," the United States and China have a relationship that was truly unimaginable two generations ago. At the same time, there are some Americans who believe that China's strategic interests are incompatible with those of the United States.

The Council on Foreign Relations established an Independent Task Force to take stock of the changes under way in China today and to evaluate what these changes mean for China and for the U.S.-China relationship. Based on its careful assessment of developments in the country and China's likely future trajectory, the Task Force recommends that the United States pursue a strategy focused on the integration of China into the global community and finds that such an approach will best encourage China to act in a way consistent with U.S. interests and international norms. The Task Force concludes with a series of recommendations aimed to reinforce recent efforts to deepen U.S.-China cooperation. The overall message is that while the United States should not turn a blind eye to the economic, political, and security challenges posed by China's rise and should be clear that any aggressive behavior on China's part would be met with strong opposition, U.S. strategy toward China must focus on creating and taking advantage of opportunities to build on common interests in the Asia–Pacific region and as regards a number of global concerns.

On behalf of the Council on Foreign Relations, I wish to thank Task Force Chairs Carla A. Hills and Dennis C. Blair, who contributed their considerable expertise and unwavering commitment to this important project. The Council is also indebted to the individual Task Force members, whose input and insight strengthened the final product immeasurably. I also wish to thank the Council's former Cyrus Vance Fellow in Diplomatic Studies Evans J.R. Revere, who began this project, and Hitachi International Affairs Fellow Frank Sampson Jannuzi, who, despite being on the other side of the world, skillfully brought it to fruition.

Richard N. Haass
President
Council on Foreign Relations
April 2007

Acknowledgments

Any effort to take stock of the changes under way in China and what they portend for U.S.-China relations must overcome at least two hurdles. First, China refuses to sit still and be evaluated. Over the past sixteen months, the work of the Independent Task Force on U.S. policy toward China, sponsored by the Council on Foreign Relations, was complicated by dramatic changes in China's relations with its neighbors, domestic policy adjustments by Beijing, a North Korean nuclear test, and China's use of a missile to destroy one of its own satellites, to name but a few important developments. China and its East Asian neighbors are not at equilibrium, and the Task Force had to be nimble. Second, China commands a special place in the American political imagination, eliciting strong views and making consensus judgments difficult. The Task Force could not have reached any meaningful conclusions about China and U.S.-China relations without the skillful, balanced, and patient leadership of its Chairs, Carla A. Hills and Dennis C. Blair. They both brought enormous experience, wisdom, and zeal to this project, and it has been a great pleasure to work with them.

The Task Force is truly independent, but we wish to acknowledge the many contributions of those on whom we have called for support, "reality checks," and guidance. Lee Feinstein, executive director of the Council's Task Force program, shepherded the process from beginning to end, helping the group stay on target and reminding the Task Force to reach for clear findings supported not only by argument, but also by evidence. At the Council, Elizabeth C. Economy, C.V. Starr senior fellow and director for Asia studies; Sebastian Mallaby, director of the Maurice R. Greenberg Center for Geoeconomic Studies; and Adam Segal, Maurice R. Greenberg senior fellow for China studies; all graciously lent their expertise to the enterprise. Other Council colleagues were also a huge help. Lindsay Workman and Samm Tyroler-Cooper handled all of the logistics and research needs. Communications staff Lisa Shields and Anya Schmemann got the report into the right hands, and got the word out. Nancy E. Roman and her staff at the Council's Washington program organized the rollout event in Washington, DC, and Irina A. Faskianos arranged for the Task Force to brief a group of academics on its work. Council Publications staff Patricia Lee Dorff and Lia C. Norton edited, formatted, and otherwise whipped the draft into shape.

Evans J.R. Revere, formerly the Council's Cyrus Vance fellow in diplomatic studies and now the president of the Korea Society, got this project off the ground and compiled the Task Force's key findings and policy recommendations, helping to focus its later discussions. Every member contributed to the deliberations, but the Task Force wishes to extend special thanks to Harry Harding, Nicholas R. Lardy, Thomas J. Christensen, Virginia Ann Kamsky, Stephen A. Orlins, and James C. Mulvenon, who briefed the group, sparking lively debates. Alan D. Romberg also deserves special thanks for his meticulous editorial eye.

The Task Force is grateful to the distinguished scholars and specialists we turned to many times for ideas and advice. Special thanks to Bonnie S. Glaser, senior associate at the Center for Strategic and International Studies, and Robert A. Kapp, former president of the U.S.-China Business Council, for their sage guidance. I am also personally indebted to Elise Carlson Lewis, vice president of membership and fellowship affairs at the Council on Foreign Relations, who manages the International Affairs Fellowship Program that has made possible my year of study and teaching in Japan.

The Task Force is particularly grateful to Richard N. Haass, president of the Council on Foreign Relations, for appreciating that for all of the challenges confronting the United States in other parts of the world, U.S.-China relations remain critical for the future of the United States and, indeed, for the planet.

Finally, the Council on Foreign Relations expresses its thanks to the Starr Foundation and to David M. Rubenstein for their generous support of the Task Force program.

Frank Sampson Jannuzi
Project Director

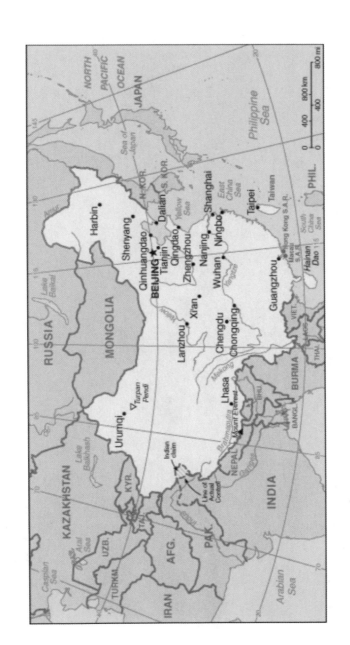

Source: Central Intelligence Agency.

List of Acronyms

APEC	Asia-Pacific Economic Cooperation
ARF	Association of Southeast Asian Nations Regional Forum
ASEAN	Association of Southeast Asian Nations
CCP	Chinese Communist Party
CNOOC	China National Offshore Oil Corporation
COCOM	Coordinating Committee
CSEPA	Chinese State Environmental Protection Administration
CSIS	Center for Strategic and International Studies
CSR	corporate social responsibility
DPP	Democratic Progressive Party
ETIM	East Turkistan Independence Movement
EU	European Union
FDI	foreign direct investment
GAO	Government Accountability Office
GDP	gross domestic product
GPA	Government Procurement Agreement
ICBM	intercontinental ballistic mussile
IEA	International Energy Agency
IIE	Institute for International Economics
IPR	intellectual property rights
NCND	"neither confirm nor deny"
NDEA	National Defense Education Act

NGO	nongovernmental organization
OECD	Organization for Economic Cooperation and Development
OIE	World Organization for Animal Health
PAROS	Prevention of an Arm's Race in Outer Space
PASSEX	passing exercise
PLA	People's Liberation Army
PRC	People's Republic of China
SAIC	State Administration for Industry and Commerce
SAREX	search-and-rescue exercise
SARS	severe acute respiratory syndrome
SCO	Shanghai Cooperation Organization
SOE	state-owned enterprises
TAR	Tibet Autonomous Region
TRA	Taiwan Relations Act of 1979
WHO	World Health Organization
WIPO	World Intellectual Property Organization
WMD	weapons of mass destruction
WTO	World Trade Organization

Task Force Report

Introduction

A Policy Consensus under Strain

President Richard M. Nixon reached out to the People's Republic of China thirty-five years ago to advance U.S. strategic interests by balancing the Soviet Union and reinforcing the split between two former communist allies. Nixon and his national security adviser, Henry Kissinger, briefed the Chinese on Soviet forces arrayed against China and also discussed the Vietnam War and Taiwan.[1] Nixon and Kissinger sought to change the global U.S. stance from confrontation to détente and to extricate the United States from the Vietnam War. Their mission shifted the globe's geopolitical landscape.[2]

For nearly two decades, U.S. policy toward China (and Taiwan) remained rooted in the strategic interests that led Nixon to Beijing during the Cold War. This policy has commonly been known as "engagement." Through engagement, China's relationship with the United States has been transformed from one characterized by near-constant antagonism to one in which dialogue and cooperation have become common.

---

[1] According to recently declassified records of Nixon's February 22, 1972, meeting with Chinese Premier Zhou Enlai, Nixon provided private assurances that the United States would not support any Taiwan independence movement, and also asserted that Taiwan was part of China and that Washington would support any "peaceful resolution of Taiwan issues" that could be negotiated. The records are available online at http://www.gwu.edu/~nsarchiv/nsa/publications/DOC_readers/kissinger/nixzhou/index.html.

[2] For a discussion of this, see Margaret Macmillan, *Nixon and Mao: The Week That Changed the World* (New York: Random House Publishing Group, 2007), pp. xvi–xxii.

And through its engagement with the world, China itself is also transforming. The normalization of U.S.-China relations during the Carter administration helped create an international environment conducive to the launch in the late 1970s of China's economic reforms under the leadership of Deng Xiaoping. Engagement helped integrate China into a virtual "alphabet soup" of multilateral organizations, including the World Trade Organization (WTO), the Association of Southeast Asian Nations Regional Forum (ARF), and the Asia Pacific Economic Cooperation (APEC) forum, to name but a few. China has become a player on the world stage.

In the security realm, China used to stand aloof. Today it is connected. China has acceded to various arms control treaties and related nonproliferation organizations, and it has gradually conformed its domestic regulations to their requirements. China has joined the Nuclear Nonproliferation Treaty, the Chemical Weapons Convention, and the Nuclear Suppliers Group; agreed to abide by the limits of the Missile Technology Control Regime; and signed the Comprehensive Nuclear Test Ban Treaty.

China's integration has not been linear or without turmoil. When China's government brutally suppressed protesters in Tiananmen Square in June 1989, the United States responded by severing its security ties to Beijing and placing human rights concerns prominently on the agenda in U.S.-China relations. And when the Soviet Union collapsed two years later, the Cold War rationale used by Nixon to justify engagement with China—the "strategic triangle"—evaporated, shifting the focus of U.S.-China relations toward new areas, including nonproliferation, trade, and regional security.

Today, the geopolitical terrain is shifting again, altered by the emergence of China as a major power in a world dominated by the United States since the collapse of the Soviet Union. Despite the overall success of engagement in helping to shape China's interests in ways desired by the U.S. government, U.S. political support for engagement is under strain. As China's economic and military power grows, there is considerable uncertainty about its future course. China's development has raised concerns about the implications for America's economic health, security, and global political influence. Many Americans are not confident that China's strategic interests are still compatible with those of the United States and argue that engagement does not sufficiently protect the United States against a China that could emerge as a threatening adversary in the future.[3] Others have concluded as Senator Jesse Helms (R-NC) did in the late 1990s: "Those who support economic engagement with China must recognize it for what it is—appeasement. . . .We must have a new approach."[4]

Popular opinions of China have actually *improved* since the low point of the Tiananmen tragedy in 1989. A 2004 Zogby poll revealed that 59 percent of Americans held a "favorable" view of China and only 24 percent saw China as a serious economic threat.[5] Most books and articles on China are consistent with this popular view. As was the case a few decades ago with U.S. treatment of Japan, however, there are also highly publicized alarmist polemics describing the inevitability of war with China.

What are the sources of this unease? China's rapid economic development, accompanied by an enormous and growing trade surplus with the United States, is a major factor. The economic challenge posed by China has become synonymous with the larger challenge of globalization, especially the pressures created by competition with low-wage economies.

Second, political liberalization and respect for human rights in China has lagged behind expectations and what the Chinese people themselves deserve. Successive U.S. administrations have argued that maintaining normal relations with China would promote both economic *and* political reforms there. This sentiment was clearly articulated by President George W. Bush's future national security adviser and secretary of state, Condoleezza Rice, in February 2000: ". . . trade in general can open up the Chinese economy and, ultimately, its politics too. This view

---

[3] Khalizad, et al., *The United States and a Rising China: Strategies and Military Implications* (Santa Monica, CA: The RAND Corporation, 1999). For a more recent assessment, see Bates Gill, *Rising Star: China's New Security Diplomacy* (Washington, DC: Brookings Institution Press, 2007).

[4] Jesse Helms, "Two Chinese States," *Washington Post,* March 31, 2000.

[5] The Committee of 100, a national nonpartisan organization, commissioned the poll, which was conducted by Zogby in 2004. Poll results are drawn from the Committee of 100 website, www.committee100.org, accessed on February 1, 2007.

requires faith in the power of markets and economic freedom to drive political change, but it is a faith confirmed by experiences around the globe."[6] Yet the Chinese Communist Party (CCP) has maintained its authoritarian grip, restricting organized political activities and suppressing criticisms directed at the basic principles underlying CCP control, in sharp contrast to the considerable leeway it gives entrepreneurs in the economic arena. President Bill Clinton expressed frustration with China's human rights record when he engaged in a spirited debate with Chinese Premier Jiang Zemin in Beijing in June 1998. President Clinton argued that "stability in the twenty-first century will require high levels of freedom" in China. President George W. Bush has amplified this view. Despite such pressure, political reform has stalled, and according to the State Department's human rights report, there has been some backsliding in respect for international norms of human rights under President Hu Jintao.[7]

Third is the issue of China's expanding economic and political influence in Southeast Asia, the Middle East, Africa, and Latin America, and the consequences for U.S. interests. Critics of engagement argue that rather than working to maintain stability and reinforce the global order, China is actually seeking to displace the United States from the leadership role it has played since the end of World War II, rewrite the rules of the institutions the United States helped found, and undercut U.S. leverage in dealing with states such as North Korea, Iran, and Sudan (where China has used its seat on the UN Security Council to help block strong action to stop mass killings).

Fourth, China's economic growth has provided Beijing the wherewithal to modernize its military—a decade of defense budget growth, including an 18 percent increase for 2007—and even develop a robust space program. This has given rise to concerns in some quarters that China will soon emerge as a military "peer competitor" of the United States; a nation able to contest U.S. primacy in East Asia and project

---

[6] Condoleezza Rice, "Campaign 2000: Promoting the National Interest," *Foreign Affairs*, January/February 2000.

[7] See the following report, *China: Country Reports on Human Rights Practices* (Bureau of Democracy, Human Rights, and Labor), March 8, 2006, available at http://www.state.gov/g/drl/rls/hrrpt/2005/61605.htm.

power around the globe. The secrecy that enshrouds China's defense establishment helps fuel this anxiety.

Finally, the challenges posed by an ascendant China come at a time when the United States is immersed in a global campaign against terrorism and carrying the burdens of major military and political commitments aimed at achieving stability in Afghanistan and Iraq. These priorities have absorbed energy and resources at a time when clear and consistent policy direction is needed to rebuild a national consensus on how best to deal with China.

Taking stock of U.S.-China relations, the Task Force finds that China's overall trajectory over the past thirty-five years of engagement with the United States is positive. Growing adherence to international rules, institutions, and norms—particularly in the areas of trade and security—marks China's global integration. China has also become more attentive to U.S. views, particularly on issues that China understands are central to the interests of the United States but less important to its own. Our assessment is based not only on China's actions, but also on the power of the forces that have been unleashed in China as a consequence of engagement. International trade and foreign investment, the entrepreneurial spirit, the Internet, judicial training, treaty commitments, foreign travel, greater educational opportunities, and growing numbers of NGOs—all of these factors are putting pressure on the Chinese government to improve rule of law, enhance transparency and accountability, and better adhere to international norms. China's interests are increasingly intertwined with the fabric of the international community of which it is an inseparable part. China has a growing stake in the future of an international system that has helped it prosper and grow strong.

Yet even as China has become more integrated, it has also grown more powerful and assertive in the international arena, bringing into sharper focus those areas where China's interests and those of the United States diverge, including how best to pursue certain nonproliferation objectives; respect for human rights (especially political liberty, freedom of speech, and religious freedom); and the limits on sovereignty to protect a nation from outside intervention when that nation grossly violates international norms (e.g., Sudan). The United States should not be satisfied with the state of U.S.-China relations or indifferent to the economic, security, and political challenges presented by

China as an emerging great power. U.S. strategy toward China must provide tools and create opportunities to narrow differences as well as build on common interests.

Future U.S. Strategy toward China

Former Deputy Secretary of State Robert B. Zoellick gave the most thorough explanation of the Bush administration's approach toward China in a speech to the National Committee on U.S.-China Relations on September 21, 2005. Zoellick called on China to act as a "responsible stakeholder" in global affairs. Zoellick's carefully crafted statement was laudable for its clarity and candor. Zoellick pledged continuing U.S. efforts to integrate China into the international community, but he also stated that the United States would "hedge" its security bets against the possibility that China might become aggressive or otherwise prove hostile to U.S. interests.

In Beijing, as in Washington, support for globalization is under strain. Peaceful development is China's official policy, but some Chinese debate U.S. intentions and how best to balance their relations with the United States. Some officials interpret U.S. military deployments to Central Asia and outreach to Mongolia and Vietnam as part of an effort to encircle China. Beijing remains deeply concerned about the implications of U.S. arms sales to Taiwan, and military planners also fear that the United States in a crisis might seek to cut off China's access to strategic commodities. Some Chinese strategists argue that the United States is seeking to thwart China's economic development, citing U.S. export controls on advanced technologies. Others believe that U.S. calls for democracy betray an intention to foment social upheaval in China—a "color revolution" like those in Eastern Europe. Finally, although the Chinese people are generally favorably disposed toward Americans—as Americans are toward the Chinese—they remember and resent the U.S. bombing of their embassy in Belgrade in 1999, the fact that the United States is seen as having blocked China's bid to host the Olympics in 2000, and the fatal collision of a Chinese fighter plane and an American electronic surveillance aircraft in 2001.

In recommending an appropriate overall *strategy* for advancing U.S.-China relations in the era of globalization, the Task Force considered the expansion of areas of common interest between the United States and China, the differences and mutual suspicions that linger, and the uncertainties about China's future.

The Task Force finds U.S. strategy toward China should be focused on an affirmative agenda of integrating China into the global community, thereby helping to shape China's self-interest in ways that will build on areas of existing cooperation and create new opportunities for collaboration on regional and global challenges. Integration is a responsible course involving a blend of engaging China on issues of mutual concern, weaving China into the fabric of international regimes on security, trade, and human rights, and balancing China's growing military power. These three dimensions can and should be pursued at the same time using all instruments of national power, governmental and nongovernmental. The United States cannot be certain of China's course—the path down the river—even though it can often discern the riverbanks between which China's leaders must navigate. U.S. strategy toward China must make allowances for this uncertainty. Elements of "hedging" will be present in such a strategy, as they are in U.S. relations with other nations, to discourage China from counterproductive policies and to provide a fallback if persuasion fails. There is no reason to hide this fact from China. But the emphasis should be focused on building a close, candid, and cooperative relationship with China in order to advance common interests and constructively address differences.

In the pages that follow, the Task Force attempts to take stock of the changes under way in China and what they portend for it, and, more specifically, for U.S.-China relations. The Task Force report concludes with policy recommendations designed to implement a consistent and positive strategy of integration, an approach the Task Force believes will best allow the United States to advance its interests with a dynamic China marked by growing economic and military power and enormous domestic challenges.

China's Economic and Social Transformation

China is so large, populous, and complex that almost anything one might assert about China is "true." China is modern and ancient. Communist and capitalist. Rich and poor. Reforming and resisting change. Homogenous and diverse. Repressive and freewheeling. Conservative and revisionist. Passive and aggressive. Strong and weak.

Understanding China is also complicated by the fact that China is changing rapidly. If the United States is to develop sound policies to advance its interests with China, it must identify the essential truths about China and correctly gauge the direction and speed of the changes under way. One place to start is by examining China's economic growth and what it has wrought.

Sustained Economic Expansion Liberates Millions from Poverty

China is in the midst of a strong and steady economic expansion unprecedented in scale, directly affecting the lives of one-fifth of the earth's population. Since 1988, China's annual gross domestic product (GDP) growth has averaged 8.5 percent. Based on its official exchange rate, China's GDP was $2.5 trillion in 2006, fourth in the world after the United States, Japan, and Germany. Adjusted for purchasing power parity, China's GDP was roughly $10 trillion in 2006, second to the

United States, although it should be noted that this ranking greatly overstates China's influence in the world economy. Trade and investment flows are made and measured at exchange rates. China's per capita GDP based on purchasing power parity ($7,600 in 2006) ranked just 109th out of 229 countries,[8] but this was still ten times higher than it was in the mid-1980s. China is on track to double per capita GDP during the period 2000–2010.

China's economic record compares favorably to the performance of other countries in similar stages of development. From 1955 until 1972, Japan's real GDP grew at an average rate of 10 percent per year, although the growth was punctuated by brief recessions. By comparison, Japan's longest period of postwar economic expansion lasted fifty-seven months between November 1966 and July 1970.

The benefits of China's economic growth have been broadly, if unevenly, spread across the population, benefiting citizens from every province and in nearly every walk of life. For the average Chinese, growth means enhanced quality of life. Some four hundred million people have been lifted out of absolute poverty. Life expectancy has reached seventy-two years, and the child mortality rate (under five years of age) shrank from 120 for every one thousand births in 1970 to just thirty-one in 2004. Illiteracy has been cut by two-thirds: Today 93 percent of Chinese are literate, although illiteracy remains a problem, particularly in rural areas where children leave school early to find work. In the decade ending in 2004, the number of Chinese households owning color televisions increased by nearly half. The Chinese cell phone market topped 400 million users in 2006, and China's Ministry of Information Industry predicts that the number of subscribers in China will grow by another 250 million over the next five years.

The engine for China's growth is its private sector. The inefficient state sector, though still relevant, is shrinking, from some 300,000 state-owned enterprises (SOEs) a decade ago to around 150,000 today, with a corresponding 40 percent decline in state-sector employees. The private sector is growing, fueled by high domestic savings and a process the Chinese call *gaige kaifang*, "reform and opening up," launched by

---

[8] See https://www.cia.gov/cia/publications/factbook/rankorder/2004rank.html, last updated March 15, 2007.

Deng Xiaoping in the late 1970s. Opening up has fostered competition and spurred foreign direct investment (FDI). China now routinely ranks first or second (behind the United States) in attracting FDI. Since entering the WTO in 2001, China has reduced its tariffs and eliminated most quotas, forcing domestic firms to become more efficient and boosting productivity.

China has also augmented outlays on research and development and higher education in an effort to spur innovation and move beyond its reliance on producing labor-intensive, low-technology products. Access to higher education has expanded dramatically. China's science and technology workforce now includes about 2.25 million scientists and engineers, and 23,500 doctorates awarded by Chinese universities in 2004 (70 percent of the total doctorates) were in science-related subjects. More multinational corporations are moving higher-level work to China, not just manufacturing, allowing China to build a more modern industrial economy. However, according to a study by the Institute for International Economics (IIE) and the Center for Strategic and International Studies (CSIS), China still spends less than one-tenth of what the United States does on research and development and only 10 percent of its scientific graduates are internationally competitive.[9] And although China's university system has grown and improved considerably over the past thirty years, *Newsweek*'s "Top 100 Global Universities" does not include any Chinese schools. The *Times Higher Education Supplement* (UK) lists only two Chinese universities in the top fifty: Beijing University at fourteenth and Tsinghua University at twenty-eighth. The quality of some schools is so poor that many of the graduates cannot find jobs and others cannot land the jobs for which they think they are qualified.

The Task Force finds that China's market-driven economic reforms are delivering real benefits to the Chinese people and that China is modernizing at a startling rate, but that China is unlikely to rival the United States or other modern industrialized countries in overall technological innovation for the foreseeable future.

---

[9] Bergsten, et al., *China: The Balance Sheet: What the World Needs to Know about the Emerging Superpower* (Washington, DC: Center for Strategic and International Studies and Institute for International Economics, 2006), p. 4.

Enormous Challenges Remain

For all of China's recent success, enormous challenges remain. Almost one-third of China's manufacturing output is still produced by inefficient state-owned enterprises. Completing reforms of the state sector will not be easy, as the most productive and well-managed firms have already been privatized. Perhaps the greatest challenge is the continuing poverty that afflicts hundreds of millions of Chinese. As noted in *China: The Balance Sheet,* "China is the world's fourth largest economy, but its per capita income is ranked around 100th in the world, making China the first 'poor' global superpower in history."[10] About four hundred million Chinese still live on less than two dollars a day and lack basic needs such as clean water and adequate housing. China's poor are as numerous as the entire population of the United States and Japan combined. In stark contrast to the glittering streets of Shanghai, much of China remains mired in poverty.

Apart from addressing the needs of the poor, China's leaders know they must also confront a host of new challenges, many of them the products of economic growth. Environmental, demographic, and public health trends, widening income disparities, a growing middle class clamoring for more responsive and accountable government, lingering ethnic and religious grievances, and endemic corruption all threaten China's economic health and political stability. China's leaders are also aware that they face these challenges at a time when their own legitimacy and that of the CCP depend increasingly on sustaining economic growth.

Environmental Degradation

China's environment is deteriorating, adversely affecting its economy and overall quality of life. In its frantic push for growth, China has chosen short-term economic development over environmental preservation, and as a result, air and water quality have been compromised. Cheap cashmere on the shelves of American department stores means hillsides denuded of grass in Inner Mongolia. China is losing roughly 1,700 square miles of formerly productive agricultural land annually to

---

[10] Ibid.

desertification. The Chinese State Environmental Protection Adminis-tration (CSEPA) acknowledges that environmental degradation costs China 8 percent to 13 percent of its annual GDP—the push for growth is not succeeding as well as it might were China's policies more balanced.[11] Water shortages alone cost $42 billion per year in lost industrial and agricultural output, according to Chinese government estimates.

China's air quality is poor, especially in urban areas, and is getting worse. Sixteen of the world's twenty most air-polluted cities are in China. China relies on coal-fired power plants to generate electricity, and it is opening a new coal-burning plant every week. The number of vehicles is set to increase from 25 million today to 100 million by 2020, contributing to ground-level ozone and nitrogen dioxide (NO_2) pollution. China's economy is truly 24/7; China is the only industrial nation on earth that does not experience the "weekend effect"—the lower concentrations of NO_2 detected by satellites on the weekend as compared to workdays.[12] Construction projects further degrade air quality. The average concentration of fine-particle pollution in Beijing is seven times the ambient air quality standard recommended by the U.S. Environmental Protection Agency. The World Health Organization (WHO) estimates that air pollution is responsible for four hundred thousand premature deaths in China every year. Pollution can also exacerbate infectious diseases that have their origin in China, as a recent study on the mortality rate of severe acute respiratory syndrome (SARS) suggests.[13]

Like clean air, clean water is in short supply. China's per capita water supply is just 25 percent of the global average. The Yellow River, cradle of Chinese civilization, no longer reliably flows to the ocean, sucked dry by new industries and burgeoning cities. Two-thirds of China's cities do not have enough water to meet their needs, and

---

[11] This estimate, from Pan Yue, the vice minister of China's State Environmental Protection Administration, is based on what it would cost to remedy the damage done to China's environment. Pan Yue's commentary, "Environmental Costs in China," is available online at http://www.env-econ.net/2006/12/reducing_enviro.html.

[12] Paul J. Crutzen, *Frontiers in Ecology and the Environment*, September 2006.

[13] Daniel S. Greenbaum and Robert O'Keefe, *"China's Environmental Health Challenges,"* *Frontiers in Ecology and the Environment*, September 2006.

experts warn that by 2030, per capita water resources will drop to 1,760 cubic meters, which is perilously close to the 1,700-cubic-meter level that is the internationally recognized benchmark for water shortages. Already, more than three hundred million people in China drink water contaminated by chemicals and toxins, and six hundred million have water supplies contaminated by human and animal waste. Nearly 50 percent of river water in China is unsuitable for agriculture or industry.

China's impact on the environment is not contained within its borders. The World Wildlife Fund reports that the lower reaches of the Yangtze River are so polluted that the river is now the largest source of pollution of the Pacific Ocean. China will surpass the United States as the world's leading emitter of carbon dioxide (CO_2) by 2009, according to a recent study by the International Energy Agency. China is already the world's largest emitter of sulfur dioxide (SO_2), thanks to its reliance on coal for power. SO_2 generated in China causes acid rain in Korea and Japan. China is also the world's largest source of unnatural emissions of mercury. Each year China spews more than 500 tons of mercury into the air, mostly from coal-burning power plants, in contrast to the 120 tons emitted by the United States. Over 30 percent of mercury found in ground soil and waterways in the United States comes from other countries, with China the probable number-one source.

The Task Force finds that if China fails to adopt more sustainable environmental practices and enforce stringent environmental protections, China will severely jeopardize its own economic future and undermine global efforts to reduce global warming, preserve biodiversity, and protect fisheries.

Unfavorable Demographic Trends

China's one-child-per-family policy, combined with improvements in health care, has had two negative demographic side effects: the male-female birth ratio has become skewed because a preference for male children sometimes results in the abortion of female fetuses, and China's society is rapidly aging. The aging population will make it difficult to provide social security and health benefits to the elderly without bankrupting the state or impoverishing working people. Chinese say they fear the country "will grow old before it grows rich."

- In most societies, there are between 102 and 106 male births for every 100 female births. In China, that number is estimated to be as high as 118.
- Chinese researchers say that there are 41 million more males than females out of China's total population of 1.3 billion, and the gap is widening.
- The peak working-age population in China will be seen in the year 2015. The dependency ratio will increase rapidly over the following quarter century.
- The international programs division of the U.S. Census Bureau estimates that roughly seven out of one hundred Chinese are currently over the age of sixty-five. Within the next thirty years, that proportion is set to more than double.
- By 2030, elderly Chinese will number 240 million—slightly more than the entire population of Indonesia.

Widening Inequalities and Social Unrest

Although nearly every region of China is experiencing economic growth, there is a growing gap between rich and poor. In a nation that once prided itself on egalitarianism, more than three hundred thousand millionaires now control some $530 billion in assets.[14] Coastal provinces have income levels ten times that of China's poorest province, and the urban-rural income ratio is more than three to one. The widening gulf has sparked a largely unregulated migration to urban areas, with perhaps as many as 160 million laborers residing illegally in cities. The gap also causes resentment in poorer areas, particularly when new investment drives villagers off land that they have farmed for generations or lays claim to scarce water and power resources. Many members of China's new elite are members of the Chinese Communist

---

[14] According to Merrill Lynch & Co., Inc. and the Boston Consulting Group.

Party who enjoy preferential access to economic opportunity and have parlayed their access to power into riches. The CCP has seen its reputation tarnished as more Chinese regard themselves the victims of official neglect, corruption, and exploitation, including excessive taxes and involuntary and inadequately compensated land confiscation. As a result, China's economic development has been accompanied by a significant increase in social unrest. Widespread public incidents of unrest are remarkable in a system that prides itself on political and social control, but according to China's Ministry of Public Security, China experienced seventy-four thousand "mass incidents" in 2004, up from ten thousand ten years earlier. Some recent protests have involved as many as one hundred thousand people, the largest demonstrations since the Tiananmen tragedy of 1989.

China's leaders are trying to extend economic opportunity to less developed regions and build a "safety net" for the poor. These efforts (described below) are still in their early stages, and it is too soon to evaluate their full impact. *Nonetheless, the Task Force finds that for the foreseeable future, there will be huge numbers of poor people in China, and the gap between China's rich and poor may become more pronounced even as economic growth continues to lift millions out of poverty.* Whether the social unrest spawned in part by widening inequality will worsen will depend on the effectiveness of government policies designed to redress poverty and to process grievances, which in large measure will determine whether the poor in China believe they are treated justly by the government. *Failure to loosen the political system to allow for peaceful dissent and a means of redress, accountability, and transparency will heighten the risk that disaffected Chinese will take to the streets.*

Clamoring Middle Class

Pressure on the government is not only coming from the poor and the disadvantaged, but also from the growing rural and urban middle class. China's citizens are calling for clean water, better housing, better health care and education, more political participation, and more accurate information. Chinese are traveling and studying abroad, and they are not always pleased by the comparison between their country and its more economically advanced and democratic neighbors. Some are registering their dissatisfaction by publishing articles critical of the conduct of the government, launching Internet blogs discussing sensitive topics, filing lawsuits to challenge official misconduct, and even mounting efforts to unseat unpopular local officials using direct elections.[15]

The demands of China's middle class are manifest in the growth of nongovernmental organizations (NGOs). There are now roughly 285,000 registered NGOs, including more than 2,000 dedicated to environmental protection. NGOs working in the fields of public health, education, and services for the disabled are generally welcomed by the government, but Chinese authorities, particularly at the local level, remain quite wary of NGOs with programs in the areas of human rights, labor law, and religious freedom. NGOs are sometimes hobbled by red tape or by policies designed to stifle certain kinds of associations. A Chatham House study of NGOs in China reported that internal guidelines effectively prohibit the formation of NGOs by "specific social groups," such as migrant laborers, laid-off workers, or ex-servicemen.[16]

Benefiting from the reforms introduced by the leadership over the past thirty years, the Chinese people today are more self-reliant than at any other time during the Communist era. They procure their own housing, compete for jobs, pay tuition and health care costs, and finance their own retirement. In short, they have become largely independent actors responsible for their own futures rather than the beneficiaries of an all-providing Communist system. The people have chosen to trade economic security for greater economic opportunity and personal responsibility. Implicit in the new social contract is the notion that China's citizens will play a more active role in governance, and that the CCP must be more responsive. But it is unclear whether the people and the government acknowledge the existence of this new contract, and if they do, whether they accept its inherent mutual obligations.

---

[15] For a discussion of trends in China's village-level and township-level elections, see Dr. Baogang He, "How Democratic Are Village Elections in China?" *National Endowment for Democracy*, and Dong Lisheng and Jørgen Elklit, "China: Village Committee Elections: First Steps on a Long March?" *ACE Electoral Knowledge Network*, March 14, 2006, available at http://aceproject.org.

[16] Yiyi Lu, "The Growth of Civil Society in China: Key Challenges for NGOs," Chatham House Briefing Paper, February 2005.

The Task Force finds that the most important change wrought by China's economic restructuring is in the relationship between the individual and the state. This change is not immediately visible in the empirical data describing China's emergence as a global economic power, but it may prove equally, if not more, significant in shaping China's future. In South Korea, Thailand, Malaysia, Taiwan, and Indonesia, improvements in living standards and the emergence of a middle class led to the growth of democratic institutions and the end of authoritarian rule. The initial indications are that as China's middle class grows, so too will its insistence on more effective, responsive, and accountable government, championed increasingly by nongovernmental organizations and other components of civil society. But this does not mean that a more democratic system will inevitably emerge in China because of "inexorable tides." China is following its own path of economic and political development. *In the near term, China's middle class, with its aversion to risk and its desire to preserve its own privileges, is unlikely to champion liberal democracy or development of a competitive multiparty political system, although it is likely to call for more modest reforms. The real push for liberalizing the legal system seems to be from those who aspire to middle-class status as well as those who have been adversely affected by corruption and have few legal mechanisms available to assuage their growing sense of injustice.*

Volatile Ethnic and Religious Issues

Most of China's fifty-six officially recognized minorities live in remote regions and historically have wielded little political or economic influence. But two groups—Uighur Muslims and Tibetans—occupy strategic territory and have a history of struggle against the Han majority, including periods of de facto independence from Chinese rule. Xinjiang, China's Muslim northwest semiautonomous region, and the Tibet Autonomous Region (TAR) comprise almost 40 percent of China's landmass but hold less than 5 percent of China's population. Xinjiang's twenty million Muslims live in an arid region that is home to China's largest oil reserves. Five million Tibetans (including those in the TAR and in adjoining Tibetan enclaves) live on the world's highest plateau, home not only to uranium ore and other precious metals, but also to the headwaters of four of Asia's great rivers: the Indus, Brahmaputra,

Salween, and Mekong. Tibet borders India and is estimated to hold 50 percent of the world's hydroelectric potential.

Chinese efforts to develop Xinjiang and Tibet have occurred with little meaningful participation by the local populations in decision-making. In fact, in important respects local autonomy is nowhere more constrained than in China's so-called autonomous regions and prefectures. Moreover, although living standards have improved across the board, the bulk of the profits have flowed into the pockets of Han migrants rather than local minorities, who often lack the education, skills, language ability, and official connections (*guanxi*) to compete effectively for government contracts or to cater to the needs of the newly arrived Han.

Separatist movements in both regions prompted bloody crackdowns during the early days of the People's Republic of China (PRC), and China's leaders remain vigilant against what they call "splittist" or "terrorist" movements. In 2005, roughly 130 Tibetans, mostly monks or nuns, were in prison on political grounds, and there are approximately fifty-five political prisoners in Lhasa serving sentences on the charge of "counterrevolution."[17] A campaign in Xinjiang against "extremism, splittism, and terrorism" has resulted in the detention or prosecution of thousands of Uighurs. Many have been sentenced to death. China has stepped up repression in Xinjiang since the terrorist attacks of 9/11. The U.S. decision to place the East Turkestan Independence Movement (ETIM) on its list of terrorist organizations, a move long sought by China even before 9/11, appears to have emboldened China to crack down more aggressively on Uighur separatists—even those who forswear violence—under the counterterrorism banner unfurled by the United States.

Although both Tibet and Xinjiang remain restive, absorption and assimilation, not rebellion and independence, are the trends. Westward migration by Han Chinese—some of it encouraged by China's government, some of it an organic response to economic opportunity—is rapidly making Uighurs and Tibetans minorities in their own cities, and there is no evidence that the westward migration will end. The

---

[17] See http://www.state.gov/g/drl/rls/hrrpt/2005/61605.htm.

oil industry and cross-border trade with China's Central Asian neighbors are drawing hundreds of thousands to China's northwest frontier. And the opening of the new Pinghai Tibet Railway in 2006 will almost certainly spur more Han to move permanently to Tibet.

Just as China's leaders are wary of separatist movements, they are also concerned by the growth of religious organizations, as evidenced by strict laws requiring religious groups to register with the government and restrict their social welfare activities to approved fields, such as poverty alleviation and public health. China's leaders are familiar with historical cases—the Taiping Rebellion, the Boxer Rebellion—in which faith-based organizations gave rise to zealotry and social disruption in China. The CCP bans openly religious people from party membership, even though it now welcomes entrepreneurs. China suppresses underground Protestant churches and maintains tight controls on the Catholic Church (appointing its own bishops, for example). With regard to the Catholic Church, Beijing also has a special concern, namely, the Vatican's maintenance of diplomatic relations with Taiwan. China has singled out Falun Gong practitioners for special vilification—arrests, beatings, and repression—ever since ten thousand adherents appeared outside the leadership compound in Beijing in 1999 in a silent protest to CCP policies. As Human Rights Watch noted in its 2002 report on China's campaign against Falun Gong, "For hundreds of years, China's rulers have viewed as politically most threatening those [movements] that combine elements of charismatic leadership, a high degree of organization, and mass appeal."[18]

Still, attitudes about religious belief have moderated significantly compared with the early days of the PRC and the brutal repression of the Cultural Revolution. By some estimates, there are today as many as sixty million Christians in China (compared with seventy-one million members of the CCP), and more churches are opening every year. China publishes more Bibles than any other country (forty million printed from 1980–2005), and in recent years dozens of private Protestant bookshops have opened in major cities. Buddhism is also experiencing a revival in China, as people seek to reconnect with the spiritualism

---

[18] Mickey Spiegel, "Dangerous Meditation: China's Campaign Against Falun Gong," (New York: Human Rights Watch, 2002), p.1.

that was virtually wiped out during the Cultural Revolution. China's efforts to regulate religious or quasi-religious groups today are motivated less by a specific animosity for religious expression than by a more general unease about the growth of any organization that might challenge the authority of the CCP or its legitimacy. Ironically, the more China persists in undemocratic practices, the more likely that religious organizations and beliefs will grow to fill the vacuum.

Legitimacy and Corruption

China's fourth-generation leaders[19] cannot rely, as the first generation did, on legitimacy born out of revolutionary struggle. Nor can they draw strength from having been chosen by the first generation, or by following Communist Party dogma (as did the second and third generations, respectively). China's leaders cannot lay claim to a popular democratic mandate. Direct elections instituted at the village level twenty years ago have not been adopted at higher levels where real power (especially budgetary authority) resides.[20] China's leaders are counting on sustained economic growth, gingerly laced with appeals to nationalism as well as repression, to protect the monopoly of power

---

[19] Members of the first generation—Mao Zedong, Zhou Enlai, Zhu De, and Liu Shaoqi—were generally political leaders in the creation of the Chinese Communist Party and military leaders during China's civil war. Members of the second generation—Deng Xiaoping, Hu Yaobang, Zhao Ziyang—were typically involved in the revolution in more junior roles, and went on to be the architects of China's post-Cultural Revolution modernization and opening up. Many members of this group were educated overseas. The third generation—Jiang Zemin, Zhu Rongji, Li Peng—had no role in the revolution and went to college before the Sino-Soviet split. Many studied engineering, often in the former Soviet Union. Hu Jintao, Wen Jiabao, and Zeng Qinghong represent the fourth generation. They were born in the 1940s and received a Chinese education that was disrupted by the Cultural Revolution. A few members of the fifth generation, not yet in top positions, received their education in the United States and Western Europe. In contrast with previous generations, many have backgrounds in law, finance, business, and political science rather than engineering.

[20] In 1987 the National People's Congress adopted a law providing for the direct election by secret ballot of "Villager Committees (*cunmin weiyuanhui*)." The committees fill a void created by the disintegration of communes after the Cultural Revolution. They generally oversee the administrative matters of a village, including budget management, public utilities, dispute resolution, public safety, social order and security, health issues, and local business management. A large village can consist of more than ten thousand people while small ones might only have several hundred. A typical village has one thousand to two thousand inhabitants. The formal government extends from the top in Beijing down only to the township, one organizational level above the village.

enjoyed by the CCP. This helps explain why they are so focused on securing a benign international environment in which to continue China's economic modernization, and why they have at times stoked nationalism to bolster their position at the helm. China's leaders hope to avoid the fate of the USSR and the former Soviet states affected by "color revolutions."

To do so, China's leaders will have to get a better handle on mounting corruption. Chinese citizens cite corruption as their biggest complaint about the government. Although Chinese rarely face the kind of corruption found in some societies—paying off traffic cops or paying bribes to get telephone service—corruption nonetheless intrudes on the lives of average Chinese when pension funds are stolen, public funds misused, environmental laws broken with impunity, etc. Transparency International ranked China 70 out of 159 countries in its 2006 Corruption Perceptions Index, pointing out that economic reforms, including privatization, provide officials with countless new opportunities for graft. President Hu Jintao in January 2005 told CCP leaders that corruption is the strongest factor threatening the party's ability to remain in power, and promised a serious effort to "gradually remove the soil that generates corruption." The CCP disciplined 115,000 members in 2005 for corruption and related offenses, referred fifteen thousand cases to the criminal courts for prosecution, and uncovered more than $300 million in misused public funds. China's top leaders use anticorruption campaigns strategically—to bolster public support—and tactically—to punish rivals or clear the way for protégés to advance. In a high-profile move in 2006, the Shanghai Party Secretary and Politburo member Chen Liangyu was removed from his position in connection with the misappropriation of pension funds. Chen, a protégé of former General Secretary and fellow Shanghai native Jiang Zemin, was the highest-ranking member of the Communist Party to be removed from office in more than a decade.

The Task Force finds that high-level corruption in China is endemic, and that reducing corruption will require new independent investigatory bodies and a free press that are not corrupt or subject to official intimidation. Moreover, although there are efforts at the top of the court system to effect reforms, China will have to dedicate itself to developing an independent and

professionally trained judiciary, one that is not subject to political manip-
ulation and personal connections, if it is to effectively combat corruption.
In this regard, NGOs could play an important role in training lawyers
and judges. The dilemma for China's leaders is that while they recognize
the need for an independent judiciary, they cannot create one without
building an institutional competitor to the CCP. This is a hard choice
for them and they will be led to it not by what the United States says,
but by their calculation of how best to sustain stability, growth, and
political control.

China's Leaders Respond

China's leaders are aware of the nation's many challenges and the threats
to their own legitimacy, and they are responding through a mixture
of reform and repression. Most of the reforms are in the area of economic
policy and social welfare, although elements of the legal system are also
receiving attention.

Reform

In 2004, the government launched a nationwide socioeconomic initiative, "Building a Harmonious Society." The "Harmonious Society"
program is designed to address the needs of the working poor, the
unemployed, and the elderly. The overarching goal is to reorient China's
social and economic development in the direction of greater equity
and sustainability. A highlight of this initiative was the elimination of
all agricultural taxes in 2005. Another priority has been the effort to
create a social security system. The impact of the "Harmonious Society"
program so far has been limited, but China's leaders are committed to
it. On the eve of the 2006 National People's Congress, Chinese Premier
Wen Jiabao proposed a more "people-centered" approach to development, and announced plans to put in place a new rural health care
cooperative system to cover seven hundred million farmers by 2010.

In recent years, the government has also targeted the underdeveloped
regions of the country for large-scale investments. The Great Western
Development Strategy launched in 2000 helped spur growth in Gansu,
Ningxia, Qinghai, Xinjiang, and Yunnan provinces. Since 2005, it has

been supplanted by a thrust to develop the Northeast, home to a great concentration of antiquated, state-owned heavy industries. Under the banner of "Rejuvenate the Northeast," China has invested more than $7 billion to support new highways and high-tech research corridors in Liaoning, Jilin, and Heilongjiang provinces, once known as China's "rust belt." Both the Great Western Development Strategy and the "Rejuvenate the Northeast" initiative have relied heavily on state-sponsored infrastructure projects. It is worth noting that although both are large in scale, they pale in comparison to the $60 billion to $70 billion in foreign direct investment flowing each year into China, much of it devoted to projects in coastal provinces.

Environmental protection is another area beginning to receive attention after decades of neglect. The central government has implemented a series of "green" initiatives, including the Three-North Protective Forest Program, the Natural Forest Conservation Program, and the Wetland Restoration Program. These and similar programs have achieved some limited success. For instance, China has become one of the first developing countries to remove lead from fuel, and has adopted stringent fuel efficiency and European auto emissions standards at a pace faster than the United States. But local authorities intent on sustaining economic growth have little incentive to implement China's new environmental standards, and enforcement remains lax. Moreover, the effects of development still dwarf conservation efforts.

Although many of China's reforms are focused on the economy, some touch on sensitive political and legal issues. Although large problems remain in China's criminal justice system, China has abolished the practice of "custody and repatriation," under which police used to round up and abuse peasants who had migrated illegally to cities. China has also begun to debate its reeducation through a labor (laogai) detention system that dates back to the mid-1950s. Some prominent Chinese legal scholars have called for the abolition of the laogai system, which can result in detention of up to three years without either a formal charge or finding of criminal guilt.[21] And a 2005 investigation of the criminal justice system by China's Supreme People's Procuratorate

---

[21] See for example, Liu Renwen, *Criminal Policy*, (Beijing: Chinese People's Public Security University, 2004).

revealed 3,700 cases of official abuse, including torture or illegally detaining or mistreating prisoners. Beijing acknowledged that innocent people had been put to death as a result of coerced confessions, and even admitted that organs of executed prisoners had been harvested and sold, a practice long denied by the Chinese government. The investigation itself was unusual, and the publication of its embarrassing findings even more so. Subsequent to the report, the government announced in November 2006 that the Supreme Court would review all future death penalty cases. Significant reforms are also under way in other aspects of China's legal system, including greater professionalism of the judiciary, providing citizens with rights to sue the government for certain illegalities, establishing systems of more open government information, and experimenting with techniques of public participation in administrative lawmaking.

The area where China's leaders appear most reluctant to contemplate fundamental reforms is in governance. Inside the CCP, the spirit of political reform that blossomed in the mid-1980s is moribund, and it is unlikely to be revived at the 17th Party Congress expected to convene in the fall of 2007. It went dormant on June 25, 1989, when General Secretary Zhao Ziyang, an advocate of reform, was stripped of his leadership posts and placed under house arrest for denouncing the June 4 Tiananmen Square Massacre. College campuses today are not hotbeds of political agitation. Outside the party, critics of the communist system such as former Tiananmen labor leader Han Dongfang, who has a radio program and runs a labor rights group in Hong Kong, tend to call on China to implement the rights workers have under current law. They do not advocate overthrowing the current regime, and probably would find little traction among the general public for such an idea.

Only the residents of Hong Kong, who enjoy broad political freedoms, continue to press ahead with political reform. Responding to popular pressure, Donald Tsang (recently reelected in the first competitive election for Hong Kong's chief executive) has announced his support for reform of the Basic Law of Hong Kong to allow direct election of the chief executive by universal suffrage no later than 2012, the end of his own five-year term.

The Task Force finds that China's leaders understand the many difficulties facing China and are taking steps to address issues such as economic disparities, social security, public health, legal reform, and the environment. But as U.S. lawmakers know from their own experience, the magnitude of the public policy challenges in these areas is enormous. The evidence to date suggests the Chinese government probably lacks the institutional capacity needed to enact and implement all of the necessary reforms. While experiments with greater "democracy" within the CCP seem likely, and although Hong Kong remains a bastion of democracy within China, the Task Force finds no evidence to suggest that China is planning to pursue significant democratic reforms in the near term even though many foreign analysts conclude that a free press, increased transparency, and an independent judiciary would improve the government's efficiency and reduce corruption.

Repression Still Prevalent

China's rulers have repeatedly made clear that they are willing to use the tools of an authoritarian system to limit challenges to their authority. As Freedom House concluded in its 2005 report on China's human rights conditions, "The Chinese state closely monitors political activity and uses vaguely worded, national security regulations to justify detainment or imprisonment of those who are politically active without party approval."[22] For instance, when the China Democracy Party emerged in 1998—the first time since the establishment of the PRC that an effort was made to obtain legal recognition for an opposition party— its leaders were rounded up and sentenced to prison terms of up to thirteen years on charges of subversion. It is estimated that some 850 Chinese are incarcerated for political crimes.[23] Even those trying to operate within the bounds of China's civil society sometimes run afoul of authorities. During Hu Jintao's tenure, a few environmental and public health activists have been jailed and many others intimidated after their criticisms proved embarrassing for government officials.

---

[22] Freedom House, *Freedom in the World: 2005*, (Lanham, MD: Rowman & Littlefield Publishers, Inc.), p. 145.

[23] The U.S. State Department's Country Report on Human Rights Practices in China from 2005 estimates that five hundred to six hundred people are in prison for nonviolent expression of political views under the charge of "counterrevolutionary activities," which is now a repealed crime. The same report cites that NGOs estimate another 250 are in prison for political activities connected with the Tiananmen incident. Several thousand more are being held under the State Security Law.

Particularly at the local level, officials have not shrunk from using the blunt instruments of repression. In December 2005, police in Dongzhou, Guangdong Province, violently put down a protest against the construction of a local power plant, killing several unarmed civilians. Faced with a strong international outcry, Chinese authorities at the national level intervened and ultimately arrested the local official responsible for ordering the shootings. Significantly, Dongzhou stands out among the tens of thousands of incidents of social unrest in 2005 in that it is one of only a handful known to have resulted in a significant number of casualties. Moreover, it is also significant that the villagers of Dongzhou were seeking redress against local officials who they claimed ignore or violate the policies and practices of the Chinese government. They were not challenging the legitimacy of the Chinese government. Nonetheless, the events at Dongzhou dramatize the fact that there remain limits on freedom of assembly and freedom of speech in China, and that those who cross the line are subject to intimidation, arrest, or worse.

Controlling Information

In addition to tamping down movements that might threaten CCP control, China's government is intensifying efforts to control the flow of information inside the country. China does not have a free press, and all media outlets are subject to government political controls. China examines international newsmagazines for content on sensitive topics such as Taiwan, sometimes censoring articles, and tries to regulate the political content on the Internet, employing between thirty thousand and fifty thousand screeners, censors, and investigators. When Google.cn opened in China on January 27, 2006, Google agreed to limit search results so that they did not return certain websites, including those promoting Falun Gong or examining the 1989 Tiananmen Square Massacre. Similar efforts to control information can be found on the Chinese version of Wikipedia.

Yet a visit to one of the thousands of websites on which people discuss contemporary issues reveals a wide range of opinions on everything from the latest South Korean pop star to more sensitive issues such as the Dalai Lama, official corruption, and the future of Taiwan. The ability of the Chinese people to circumvent information controls is evolving faster than the government's regulatory capacity. China's elite students are particularly adept at getting around the controls. As one Chinese graduate student at Fudan University in Shanghai proudly told a visiting senator who was dismayed at his inability to access a Western news site on the Internet, "Senator, I can show you how to do it, if you want."

It is possible for outside pressure to convince Chinese authorities to relax some media controls. In the run-up to the 2008 Olympics, for instance, China has pledged not to restrict foreign journalists reporting on the games. After the International Olympic Committee pressed China to honor this commitment, Foreign Ministry spokesman Liu Jianchao announced on December 1, 2006, that foreign journalists would no longer be subject to onerous travel restrictions and other impediments beginning on January 1, 2007, and running until October 2008. The new rules technically expire after the Olympics, but they may prove difficult to revoke, particularly with the Shanghai World Exposition scheduled for 2010.

On balance, the Task Force finds that China's attempts to control the flow of information into and within China are not keeping pace with the expanding access to information afforded by the Internet and other media. The Internet, in particular, has become a source of information and a channel for political discourse, and despite the government's zealous efforts, may yet become a virtual forum for Chinese seeking political reforms.

The Bottom Line on China's Economic and Social Transformation

While the hurdles confronting China make precise judgments about its future difficult, the Task Force concludes that for the next five to ten years, none of China's domestic challenges seems likely either to cripple growth or to divert the country from the path of economic reform and opening up. Moreover, no organized threat exists to the viability of the government, nor is one likely to emerge. In fact, most Chinese say their country is moving in the right direction. A 2006 Pew Research poll found that 81 percent of Chinese say they are "satisfied" with the way things are going, up from 72 percent in 2005, and just 48 percent in 2002.

Self-preservation will probably drive the leadership to provide more civic space for China's citizens; further reducing the likelihood that unrest will rise to a level threatening the party's control. The greatest challenge to political stability is likely to occur if China's growth begins to slow, dragged down by daunting environmental and demographic difficulties. In a country where 19 percent of the population does not identify itself as "satisfied" (and who may be unsatisfied or at best ambivalent), a number that translates into more than two hundred million people, the potential for unrest is obvious.

The Task Force finds that China needs to build stronger institutions—a professional, independent judiciary and arbitration system, freer media, and more responsive and accountable government—to contend successfully with its many domestic challenges as well as the competitive economic pressures of globalization. These institutions are important to the functioning of a market-based economy and will become even more important as China seeks to foster innovation and develop knowledge-based industries relying on high technology.

China's current leaders do not appear to share the assessment of the need for democratic reforms and greater adherence to international human rights norms to deal with the social, political, and economic challenges they face. China's overall human rights record remains poor. Nevertheless, the Task Force believes expanding U.S. cooperation with China as it strives to address its difficult domestic challenges will not only make those efforts more successful, but will also provide opportunities for individuals connected with businesses, nongovernmental organizations, think tanks, universities, international groups, and people-to-people movements both inside the United States and within China to encourage more democratic, open, and accountable institutions in China.

China's Approach to the World

Many Chinese look forward to the 2008 Summer Olympics as China's "coming out" party—the event that more than any other will signify that the Middle Kingdom has resumed its rightful place in the universe. Like its frenetic preparations for the Olympics, China's foreign policy is geared toward restoring China to a position of influence and respect in Asia and beyond. Beijing's foreign policy, like its economic and social transformation and its work on Olympic venues, is a work in progress.

China's foreign affairs have long been guided by the "Five Principles of Peaceful Coexistence."[24] They were first set forth in December 1953 by Premier Zhou Enlai. China has abided by them when it was convenient, and ignored them when deemed necessary. Today, references to the Five Principles are less frequent, but they have not been discarded. China proudly refers to the Five Principles in its relations with its Association of Southeast Asian Nations (ASEAN) neighbors, and it still points to the Five Principles to explain its refusal to impose sanctions in response to what it considers the "internal affairs" of other states, even in extreme situations such as in the mass killings in Darfur, Sudan.

---

[24] The five principles are mutual respect for sovereignty and territorial integrity, mutual nonaggression, noninterference in internal affairs, equality and mutual benefit, and peaceful coexistence.

But China's current foreign policies are based more on pragmatism than principle. China's global influence is growing, and Beijing's diplomacy is becoming more engaged and assertive. China now talks about creating a "harmonious world" (*hexie shijie*), acknowledging the global scope of China's interests. China's approach to the world includes a significant effort to advance multipolarity, attempting to reduce what it perceives to be U.S. hegemony. But China's diplomacy also includes a note of reassurance, assuring neighbors of its own peaceful intentions. China's approach to the world is focused on three broad objectives:

- Building cooperative relations with the United States while preventing the emergence of any coalition targeting China;

- Maintaining a "zone of peace" around China to enable the country to pursue its domestic agenda, especially economic strengthening, while expanding its regional influence; and

- Securing and diversifying access to natural resources (especially energy supplies) needed to fuel China's economic engine.

China's leaders consider Taiwan to be a domestic issue, but there are obvious foreign policy dimensions, particularly regarding the U.S. role in Taiwan, as well as the role of U.S. alliances in Asia.

Infusing China's foreign policy with a sense of emotion and urgency is the fact that China is seeking to reclaim its status as a respected great power as well as trying to undo a "century of shame and humiliation" brought on by Western and Japanese colonialism and imperialism. But China's ambitions are not limited to restoring its place in East Asia. China's role as Olympics host embodies the new patriotic spirit in China—proud, competitive, and *global.*

Cooperating with, and Balancing, the United States

China's leaders recognize that China's economic health and security cannot be assured if China does not enjoy good relations with the United States. Thus China's three-decade journey of reform and opening up has been characterized by expanding areas of cooperation with the United States. As President Hu Jintao said during his April 2006 visit to Washington, China and the United States ". . . share extensive, common strategic interests and there is a broad prospect for the mutually beneficial cooperation between the two countries." At the same time, China's leaders increasingly chafe at what they perceive to be American hegemony, and they work to counterbalance U.S. influence in Asia and elsewhere through their own efforts to build global economic, political, and security links. China's advocacy of "Asian-only" groupings, diplomatic outreach to Southeast Asia, Africa, and the Middle East, growing military ties to Russia, and its opposition to an enhanced role for the U.S.-Japan Alliance in East Asian security affairs (especially Taiwan), all reflect Beijing's efforts to maintain a zone of peace, to assert political leadership commensurate with China's growing economic clout, and to hedge against the possible emergence of any U.S.-led anti-China coalition. China believes this dual approach—cooperating and balancing—is most likely to create the conditions necessary for China's continued economic growth and security.

Zone of Peace

The most important objective of China's diplomacy is to create a zone of peace within which China can continue to develop its comprehensive national power. In the past twenty years, China has either formally resolved or managed to "set aside" almost all of its outstanding territorial disputes—with Russia, with India, with Vietnam, and with the five other claimants to portions of the South China Sea—and has normalized diplomatic relations with former antagonists such as the Republic of Korea. Where once China supported revolutionary movements—in Indonesia, Cambodia, the Philippines, Malaysia, Burma—China now has developed strong economic, political, and even security ties with sitting governments.

China has become more comfortable working with groups of countries on common problems, no longer concerned that the Lilliputians are intent on constraining Gulliver. China's growing confidence in multilateral settings is aptly summed up by the summit commemorating fifteen years of formal ties between China and ASEAN, held October 31, 2006, in Nanning, China. The joint statement issued at the summit focused on economic integration, but China used the summit to push a larger agenda. Premier Wen Jiabao told the assembled leaders, "We should expand military dialogue and exchanges, conduct and institutionalize cooperation" to address security-related issues such as terrorism, piracy, and other transnational crimes.

Although China has become more confident in the international arena, and its neighbors more welcoming, there remain limits on China's influence. Beijing's ambitions for regional preeminence are tempered by its neighbors' efforts collectively—through organizations such as ASEAN—and individually (through their security policies, including alliances with the United States)—to ensure themselves against risk given their uncertainties about China's intentions. A sense of unease has blossomed in many capitals as worried leaders assess the full economic and security implications of China's growth. Acknowledging this discomfort, Zheng Bijian, an influential adviser to President Hu Jintao, coined the term *zhongguo heping jueqi* (or "China's peaceful rise") in 2003 to describe China's emergence on the world scene. Zheng popularized the phrase for Western audiences in a *Foreign Affairs* article published in September/October 2005. The Western translation of Zheng's terminology had at least three defects. First, the English language expression immediately brought to mind the "rise and fall" of great powers, implying the relative decline of the United States. Second, it prompted people to ask, "China's rise might be peaceful, but what happens next?" Finally, some critics within China pointed out that to promise a peaceful rise might undermine Chinese efforts to deter Taiwan independence. Recognizing the political liabilities of the term, China's leaders shelved it in favor of the phrase "peaceful development," which is conceptually similar to but not identical with its predecessor.

The Task Force finds that China's foreign policy is focused for the near to midterm on securing the inputs for and maintaining a peaceful environment in which to achieve domestic economic and social development. China wants to avoid conflict. This focus provides opportunities for the United States to forge common understandings with China on regional security and to adopt complementary policies or even partnerships on global issues that are important to both countries, such as the war on terrorism, nuclear proliferation, and environmental protection.

Relations with Japan

Until recently, Japan stood as the notable exception to China's diplomatic effort to reassure and charm its neighbors. This was true even though economic links are strong and provide an incentive for good relations. More than 25,000 Japanese enterprises operate inside China, with 2,000 in the port city of Dalian alone. China and Japan are also major trading partners.

Despite growing economic ties, political relations have been cool for several years. This is not only a problem for Beijing and Tokyo, but also for the United States. It is difficult for the U.S.-Japan alliance to realize its full potential as an instrument of global peace and security unless China views Japan and its alliance with the United States with equanimity.

The difficulties between China and Japan are linked to questions of honor, fear, and competition for leadership and influence. Nationalism, broadly defined, is rising in both countries. China is expanding its military budget and becoming a global economic power at the same time that Japan considers revising its constitution and upgrading its military to permit an expanded role in international security affairs. It is no wonder that tensions have spiked. In recent years, China's anti-Japanese rhetoric has focused largely on the visits by former Japanese Prime Minister Junichiro Koizumi to the Yasukuni Shrine; a shrine honoring Japanese war dead, including the spirits of fourteen "Class A" war criminals from World War II.[25] Beijing has also protested Japan's publication of textbooks downplaying Japan's atrocities in China in the 1930s and 1940s. Finally, growing U.S.-Japan coordination on Taiwan policy concerns China and remains a major impediment to improved

---

[25] Koizumi reversed the policy of his predecessors to visit the shrine, which first became an issue in Japan's foreign relations in 1979 when it was revealed that the spirits of fourteen officials convicted by the International Military Tribunal for the Far East of Class A war crimes were secretly enshrined in 1978. The shrine's English-language website defends Japan's conduct before and during World War II, stating, "War is truly sorrowful. Yet to maintain the independence and peace of the nation and for the prosperity of all of Asia, Japan was forced into conflict."

Sino-Japanese relations. As one prominent Chinese academician has put it, the silver lining has rubbed off the cloud of the U.S.-Japan alliance.[26]

For its part, Japan has noted China's rapid military modernization with growing alarm. Japan has protested China's assertive military posture in the East China Sea, where China's effort to develop undersea oil and gas fields in the vicinity of disputed territory complicates a separate, long-standing territorial dispute over the Senkaku (Diaoyu) Islands. Japan also criticizes China for its poor human rights record and for what it sees as Beijing's deliberate efforts to stoke popular anti-Japanese sentiment. In the absence of genuine reconciliation, the people and governments of China and Japan continue to harbor deep-seated suspicions.

But relations have rebounded somewhat. Japan's new Prime Minister, Shinzo Abe, chose to visit Beijing and meet with President Hu Jintao last October, less than two weeks after taking office. The summit was a success. Importantly, Abe adopted the position of "neither confirm nor deny" (NCND) on Yasukuni, declining to state whether he had visited the shrine early in 2006 while chief cabinet secretary or whether he would visit the shrine while prime minister. Beijing had conditioned improvement of relations on satisfactory assurances that Abe would not visit Yasukuni. But in Japan, many of Abe's supporters had urged him to continue Koizumi's practice of visiting Yasukuni, or at least to never deny that he has a right to visit the shrine. Although Abe's NCND approach falls short of what China sought, President Hu accepted it as a way forward. Abe and Hu also announced the formation of a joint academic study group to examine questions of history and expressed their support for mutual ship visits and other steps to reduce tension and build ties. The territorial dispute will prove difficult to resolve, but a formula setting aside sovereignty considerations in favor of joint economic development may offer a way forward. At the people-to-people level, tourism, foreign study, and cultural exchanges are all flourishing. Ironically, the summit was probably given a boost by common concern over North Korea's nuclear program, underscored

---

[26] Wu Xinbo, "The End of the Silver Lining: A Chinese View of the U.S.-Japanese Alliance," *Washington Quarterly*, Winter 2006.

by North Korea's test just as Abe was winging his way from Beijing to Seoul.

The Task Force anticipates that the positive trends in Sino-Japanese economic relations combined with the recent resumption of regular high-level dialogue will lead to a gradual lessening of tension over the coming years. But the relationship clearly remains vulnerable to domestic political factors in both capitals. China's leaders sometimes find it useful to play the "history card" or the "nationalism card" with Japan, and are likely to do so again.[27] Beijing's pointed opposition to Japan's quest for a permanent seat on the UN Security Council reflects this approach. And Japan and China have not yet resolved the sensitive issues of Japan's World War II guilt and atrocities (e.g., Yasukuni shrine, school history books that tend to minimize or ignore Japanese military atrocities, "comfort women"), nor have they resolved the East China Sea territorial dispute. Moreover, security relations are still in their infancy and both Japan and China may believe it is imperative to arm against the potential threat of the other. Finally, conflicting priorities and differences over how best to thwart North Korea's nuclear ambitions could yet reverse the thaw in Sino-Japanese relations.

Relations with Taiwan

Taiwan remains a potential flash point in East Asia. It is the only issue over which leaders of both China and the United States contemplate and conscientiously prepare for armed conflict. U.S. policy toward Taiwan is articulated in the "Three Communiqués" with the PRC and the Taiwan Relations Act of 1979 (TRA). The Three Communiqués establish U.S. support for a "one China" policy[28] and also call for the

---

[27] Beijing may be somewhat chastened by its experience in April 2005 when anti-Japanese demonstrations stoked by the government got out of hand, resulting in rioting and significant economic harm.

[28] "One China" has been defined many ways by different U.S. administrations, by Congress, and by various officials. Most definitions include three core elements: 1) The PRC is the sole legitimate government of China, and the United States does not maintain official relations with Taiwan; 2) The United States does not support Taiwan independence, nor its membership in international organizations whose members are sovereign states; and 3) the United States does not challenge China's position that Taiwan is part of China, and would accept unification as long as it occurred peacefully. For a detailed discussion of the "One China" policy, see Shirley Kan, *China/Taiwan: Evolution of the "One China" Policy*, Congressional Research Service, 2006.

gradual reduction of U.S. arms sales to Taiwan consistent with the reduction of tension across the strait. The TRA states that it shall be the policy of the United States to maintain an independent capacity "to resist any resort to force or other forms of coercion that would jeopardize the security, or the social or economic system, of the people on Taiwan." The TRA also obligates the United States to "make available to Taiwan such defense articles and defense services in such quantity as may be necessary to enable Taiwan to maintain a sufficient self-defense capability." China views these U.S. commitments to Taiwan's security, especially the provision of defense goods and services to Taiwan, as an unwelcome intrusion in China's internal affairs. As it was thirty-five years ago, Taiwan remains a top concern of China's leaders, and it is never far from their minds when they consider their relations with the United States.

In the mid-1990s, China briefly flirted with setting a timetable for reunification, but abandoned that effort, along with some of the more provocative military exercises opposite Taiwan that accompanied it, in favor of a long-term strategy to constrain pro-independence sentiment, bond Taiwan economically to the mainland, and undermine support for Taiwan in Washington. Some coercive aspects of China's approach to Taiwan persist, such as its rapid missile buildup across from Taiwan. China seems satisfied to live for now with Taiwan's autonomy, provided only that Taiwan refrains from steps toward official independence. China laid down a marker in the spring of 2005, passing an "anti-secession law" that called for the use of force against Taiwan under certain conditions.[29] But the same law included conciliatory language calling for dialogue with Taiwan "on an equal footing" with "flexible and varied modalities." During the months that followed passage of the law, Beijing hosted a string of Taiwan "pan-Blue" opposition politicians, giving them the red-carpet treatment. China's approach

---

[29] Article 8 of the Anti-Secession Law adopted on March 13, 2005, states: "In the event that the 'Taiwan independence' secessionist forces should act under any name or by any means to cause the fact of Taiwan's secession from China, or that major incidents entailing Taiwan's secession from China should occur, or that possibilities for a peaceful reunification should be completely exhausted, the state shall employ non-peaceful means and other necessary measures to protect China's sovereignty and territorial integrity." Translation as it appears on the website of the Chinese Embassy, available at www.china-embassy.org.

today is marked by courtship of Kuomintang politicians (who favor eventual reunification with a democratic, prosperous mainland), economic and cultural integration, and occasional psychological intimidation of pro-independence forces, all while building up the military capacity to deter independence and strike Taiwan if diplomacy fails.

For its part, Taiwan's approach to the mainland has undergone a major shift since President Chen Shui-bian and his pro-independence Democratic Progressive Party (DPP) first came to power in 2000. Narrowly reelected in 2004, Chen continues to argue (as did his predecessor Lee Teng-hui) that Taiwan is already an independent, sovereign nation. But Chen has no popular mandate to take steps toward de jure independence through constitutional revision. Chen's presidency has been hobbled by corruption scandals and an ascendant pan-Blue opposition alliance that controls the legislature. Checks and balances in Taiwan's political system make it extremely difficult for the DPP to revise the constitution or embark on other steps that might provoke a crisis over Taiwan's political status. Pan-Blue opposition and pan-Green legislative bungling have thwarted most DPP policy initiatives, including Chen's desire to conclude an $18 billion arms purchase from the United States, a deal first authorized by the Bush administration in 2001.

Unstoppable Integration?

The more relaxed tone in cross-strait politics reflects robust economic links and the growing integration of the two societies. Two-way trade now amounts to some $65 billion each year (overwhelmingly in Taiwan's favor), and Taiwan firms have invested more than $100 billion in the mainland. Taiwan firms have even moved some sensitive high technologies to the mainland, although Taiwan still maintains significant restrictions on the transfer of its most advanced know-how to China. More than 1.2 million Taiwan citizens—almost 5 percent of the population—maintain residences in China. Cross-strait marriages are increasing. Beijing and Taipei have agreed to practical arrangements—such as more direct charter flights—as well as increasing humanitarian and economic exchange. The trend toward integration appears unstoppable.

Despite PRC concerns that Chen Shui-bian will somehow manage to advance Taiwan independence in his final year in office, this seems highly unlikely. In fact, tension across the Taiwan Strait is lower today than it has been for some time, reflecting a change of tactics by Beijing, the political troubles of the DPP, and the calming influence of Washington's approach of "dual restraint"; deterring Chinese threats of force against Taiwan while simultaneously opposing Taiwan steps toward independence. But relations are not at a point of equilibrium. Beijing remains committed to eventual reunification, and has not ruled out the use of force to accomplish that goal. For their part, the people of Taiwan see no reason to trade the autonomy and democracy they now enjoy for subordination to Beijing. Polling data consistently show that a large majority on Taiwan prefers the status quo to either reunification or independence, at least for the foreseeable future. A near-term resolution of the Taiwan issue seems highly unlikely, and U.S. involvement in any conflict cannot be ruled out.

The Task Force finds that U.S. commitments under the Three Communiqués and the Taiwan Relations Act contribute meaningfully to the maintenance of peace and stability across the Taiwan Strait. Other states in the region also view Washington's commitment to cross-strait peace and stability as an important symbol of America's strategic interest in East Asia, and would view any diminution of that interest with concern. Nevertheless, claims by both Washington and Beijing of a right to resort to force to prevent an unwanted outcome in the Taiwan Strait naturally put limits on U.S.-China bilateral military relations, even on issues and missions of common concern, and encourage each side to prepare for a worst-case scenario. Conflicting military objectives of this magnitude create their own powerful dynamic of mistrust and could even lead to a conflict neither intended nor desired by either side. Until some level of political accommodation is reached in cross-strait relations, even on an interim basis, Washington and Beijing have to continue to manage their differences on Taiwan rather than resolve them.

Securing Natural Resources

The third principal goal of China's foreign policy is to secure and diversify its access to the natural resources it needs to fuel its economic growth. Energy has become a defining dimension of this goal. China's per capita energy use is only a ninth that of the United States, but its huge population and low energy efficiency mean that China is already the second-biggest energy consumer in the world. China uses nine times more energy than Japan to produce a dollar of gross domestic product. China's dependence on imported fossil fuels is going to grow for the foreseeable future. China currently relies on the United States to provide the "public good" of safe sealanes through which most of its oil and gas imports flow. It seeks to reduce this dependency by diversifying suppliers and establishing commercial and political relation-ships—sometimes with unsavory regimes—that can weather outside pressure. China is also increasing its own blue-water naval capabilities, raising the prospect that China may someday develop an independent capability to defend vital sealanes of communication.

China's quest for energy influences many aspects of its foreign policy. After the end of the Cold War, China launched the Shanghai Five (China, Russia, Kazakhstan, Kyrgyzstan, and Tajikistan) to expand its influence in Central Asia. China hoped not only to open up cross-border trade and investment but also to ensure that the nations of Central Asia would not provide any encouragement or sanctuary to Uighur separatists. The Shanghai Five, expanded in 2001 by the addition of Uzbekistan and renamed the Shanghai Cooperation Organization (SCO), still works to combat "terrorism, separatism, and extremism" in Central Asia. But China also now looks to the SCO to help it secure oil and gas contracts and pipeline routes through SCO countries.

China's search for raw materials, especially energy, now extends far beyond its borders. China's outreach to Africa is motivated by the prospect of access to crude oil, copper, tin, timber, and other critical commodities, and it is multifaceted, with both economic and security dimensions. China's recent foray evokes the spirit of the great Chinese navigator Zheng He, who led voyages of commerce and exploration to the Indian Ocean and the east coast of Africa during the Ming Dynasty almost six hundred years ago. Two-way trade quadrupled from 2000–2005, reaching $40 billion, making China Africa's third-largest trading partner after the European Union (EU) and the United States. In 2006, Angola edged out Saudi Arabia as China's largest foreign supplier of oil. More than eighty thousand Chinese expatriates live in Africa. A steady stream of high-level delegations from Beijing toured Africa in 2006, checkbooks in hand. President Hu has visited Africa three times since becoming China's top leader.

As part of its outreach to Africa, China is active in security assistance programs. China complements its economic relations with arms sales, with Sudan, Nigeria, and Zimbabwe the major buyers. China also contributes to international peacekeeping operations in Africa, where in early 2007 it had more than 1,300 deployed in Liberia, Congo, and southern Sudan.

African leaders have mostly welcomed China's outreach. Forty-eight out of fifty-three African nations attended the China-Africa Summit in November 2006, a three-day event at which China sought to secure access to the resources it needs for its economy while promising to double aid and investment in African states.[30]

But China's new interest in Africa has also generated some criticism, even bitterness, among some African hosts. South African President Thabo Mbeki warned his fellow African leaders in December 2006 that Africa must guard against falling into a "colonial relationship" with China; in which it exports raw materials while importing manufactured goods.

No Strings Attached

China is mostly "hands off" on the internal affairs of its trading partners, eschewing political conditionality. China argues that development requires correct sequencing of priorities with economic reforms first and political liberalization a distant second (if it is mentioned at all). Beijing uses this assessment to justify an approach that also happens to coincide with China's own trade priorities and political preferences.[31]

China's "no strings attached" approach is not unique. Many other nations, including the United States, often subordinate human rights

---

[30] The only five invited guests that failed to attend—Burkina Faso, Malawi, Gambia, Swaziland, and Sao Tome and Principe—are those that still extend diplomatic recognition to Taiwan.

[31] Elizabeth Economy and Karen Monaghan, "The Perils of Beijing's Africa Strategy," *International Herald Tribune*, November 2, 2006.

concerns to other strategic interests. But China's economic relations, aid, and arms sales to countries such as Sudan, Angola, and Zimbabwe put it out of step with the United States, other members of the G8, and international financial institutions that now attempt to tie aid and investment to a nation's efforts to combat corruption and generally improve their governance practices. China makes no effort to follow international lending standards, effectively immunizing countries such as Sudan, Zimbabwe, Iran, and Burma against foreign financial pressure or multilateral sanctions regimes. China recently extended a $2 billion line of credit to Angola, for instance, despite efforts by the International Monetary Fund and World Bank to condition debt relief on anticorruption measures. In the UN Security Council, China often opposes sanctions based on human rights concerns not only because it fears how such sanctions might be wielded someday against China, but also because as a latecomer to the international energy scene, China believes it does not have the luxury of scrutinizing the human rights practices of underdeveloped energy-rich countries. Moreover, China criticizes the United States and other developed states for having a double standard—turning a blind eye to antidemocratic, poor human rights conditions in Saudi Arabia, Kazakhstan, and Libya, and "grandfathering" U.S. oil and gas investments in Burma while demanding that China halt investments in states such as Sudan. Finally, China tends to chafe at U.S.-led sanctions regimes that it regards as an unwelcome manifestation of American hegemony.

The Task Force finds that China's "no strings attached" investment and aid posture undercuts international efforts to condition aid on improved governance. It also impedes international efforts to punish governments like Sudan's for gross misconduct. China probably will continue to exploit economic and political opportunities that arise as a result of voluntary sanctions regimes, even at the risk of antagonizing Washington, unless leaders in Beijing determine that their conduct fundamentally jeopardizes PRC interests, including China's relationship with the United States or its international image.

In this regard, Iran may yet prove a test case of China's evolving international behavior. When the United States objected to China's export of cruise missiles to Iran, imposing sanctions on Chinese firms and raising the issue at the highest levels of the Chinese government,

China eventually halted the exports. Today, as the United States joins with European and other nations trying to rein in Iran's nuclear ambitions, a similar effort may be needed to convince China to weigh its energy and geopolitical interests—China gets more than 10 percent of its imported oil from Iran, and China has historically tried to forge close ties with Iran given Iran's major influence in the Middle East—against the nonproliferation goal championed by the United States and its European allies, as well as China's own core national interest of maintaining cooperative relations with the United States.[32]

---

[32] For an in-depth discussion of China's relationship with Iran, including China's support for Iran's efforts to modernize its military and oil industry infrastructure, see John W. Garver, *China and Iran: Ancient Partners in a Post-Imperial World* (Seattle: University of Washington Press, 2006).

China's Military Modernization

China's military modernization has two main drivers, one with a clear operational objective (Taiwan) and the other with a clear strategic objective (to build a modern military because China will be a modern power). In its 2005 report to Congress on China's military, the Pentagon found that China is emphasizing preparations to fight and win short-duration, high-intensity conflicts along China's periphery, particularly in the East and South China Seas, where long-standing territorial disputes hold the potential for conflict and where trade routes are of growing importance. Longer term, China's military strategy will be shaped by its growing dependence on imported oil, the presence of unstable regimes on its western and northeastern borders, and Beijing's lingering concerns about a U.S.-led containment strategy. In the 2006 Quadrennial Defense Review, the Pentagon concluded, "Of the major and emerging powers, China has the greatest potential to compete militarily with the United States and field disruptive military technologies that could over time offset traditional U.S. military advantages."[33] In January 2007, then Director of National Intelligence John D. Negroponte testified to Congress that China's modernization is driven by its aspirations for great power status and said it would continue even if the Taiwan problem were resolved.

One manifestation of China's great power aspirations is its active space program. China became the third country to put a person in

---

[33] The term "disruptive technologies" is a reference to asymmetric warfare.

space in 2003, and Beijing has established the goal of putting a person on the moon by 2024. China's investments in space systems—commercial space launch vehicles, surveillance satellites, and telecommunication satellites—all have dual-use applications. The 2006 Quadrennial Defense Review reports that China's space, air, and missile capabilities now pose a coercive threat to potential adversaries in contested areas around China. As if to demonstrate the validity of this concern, China on January 11, 2007, used a missile to destroy one of its own old weather satellites in low-earth polar orbit. It was the first time that China had successfully tested an anti-satellite system. Only Russia and the United States had previously tested such capability. The most recent U.S. test was in 1985.

China's anti-satellite test underscores the lack of transparency of China's military modernization. It took the Chinese foreign ministry more than a week to respond officially to questions about the test, and China's motives remain difficult to discern, allowing for a broad range of interpretations: a dramatic underestimation of international reactions and a corresponding breakdown in interagency coordination, a clumsy attempt to prod the United States to support treaty negotiations ongoing in Geneva for the Prevention of an Arms Race in Outer Space (PAROS),[34] or a bald "shot across the bow" announcing China's intentions to challenge America's space dominance. The test at a minimum enhanced the credibility of China's military threat to Taiwan by demonstrating a limited ability to blind the satellites that the United States would rely upon to conduct operations in the Taiwan Strait. Whatever China's true intentions—and the many competing explanations are not mutually exclusive—the test is a vivid example of how China's emerging military capabilities will complicate the strategic environment confronting U.S. forces for decades to come.

From Poverty to Plenty

Prior to 1990, the People's Liberation Army (PLA) used relatively unsophisticated equipment and had little successful combat experience.

---

[34] The administration has resisted efforts to prohibit space-based weapons and in a space policy paper published August 2006, the administration asserts the right to "freedom of action

China relied on geography and large ground forces, backed by a missile-mounted nuclear deterrent. During the 1980s, military modernization ranked last among China's four modernizations. Due to a number of factors—realization from the Gulf War of its own military backwardness, the overall advance of technology, increased wealth from its economic development, and fears of Taiwan's moves toward independence—China embarked in the mid-1990s on an across-the-board improvement program (see text box). The PLA slashed more than a million men from its ranks and began to focus on preparing for a Taiwan contingency. Military modernization—including the acquisition of advanced technologies from abroad—was integrated into China's drive to build "comprehensive national power."

Since the early 1990s, the EU and U.S. arms embargoes have effectively precluded arms purchases from the West, so China has relied on imports from Russia to fill gaps in its capabilities. These purchases include Il-76 heavy airlift, Mi-17 and Ka-28 helicopters, Sukhoi fighter aircraft, SA-10 air defense systems, Sovremenny-class destroyers armed with advanced surface-to-surface antiship missiles, and Kilo-class diesel-electric submarines. In recent years, improvements in China's defense industrial base have led to the development of high-quality indigenous weapons systems including the long-delayed F-10 fighter aircraft, similar to the U.S. F-16 and the Israeli Lavi. The one defense industrial sector in which China has consistently produced advanced and reliable systems has been ground-based missiles of all ranges. Defense technology sectors that are well integrated into the global economy (e.g., shipbuilding and information technology) have seen particular advances. Globalization and the diffusion of advanced technologies have reduced the effectiveness of regimes designed to limit the export of sensitive dual-use technologies to China.[35]

in space" and states that it will "deter others from either impeding those rights or developing capabilities intended to do so."

[35] Crane, et al., *Modernizing China's Military: Opportunities and Constraints* (Santa Monica, CA: The RAND Corporation, 2005); Medeiros, et al., *A New Direction for China's Defense Industry* (Santa Monica, CA: The RAND Corporation, 2005).

Highlights of China's Military Modernization

- From 2000–2005, China doubled its official military spending to $29 billion. Estimates adjusting for purchasing power parity, taking into account foreign arms purchases (roughly $3 billion in 2005), and including spending on paramilitary units and subsidies to defense industries put total defense sector spending in the range of $60 billion to $90 billion.*
- China has fundamentally overhauled PLA doctrine, moving from "People's War" to a doctrine emphasizing joint combat operations and advanced weapons systems in order to fight "local wars under high-technology conditions."
- The PLA is conducting increasingly sophisticated and effective training, including annual joint service amphibious exercises.
- China has reduced PLA manpower and shifted resources into acquisition of equipment (foreign and indigenous), including sophisticated space, air, maritime, command-and-control, and electronic warfare systems.
- China has liberated the PLA from its historical central role in internal security, transferring that mission (along with much obsolete equipment and redundant manpower) to the People's Armed Police.
- China has increased significantly the number, reliability, and accuracy of ballistic missiles deployed across from Taiwan to roughly eight hundred, with about one hundred new missiles being deployed each year.
- China is modernizing its nuclear forces, and is preparing to deploy a road-mobile, solid-fueled, nuclear-tipped intercontinental ballistic missile (ICBM) to replace its aging twenty liquid-fueled ICBMs, providing for the first time a credible, secure second-strike capability.

* Crane, et al., *Modernizing China's Military: Opportunities and Constraints* (Santa Monica, CA: The RAND Corporation, 2005).

The PLA's Limitations

Much of China's military strategy remains opaque, as does its military planning and budget process. China has done much to try to spell out its intentions, but intentions cannot be made entirely clear because they are not fully formed except when action is called for. China's intentions, like those of the United States, are conditional. Intentions can change rapidly in response to internal and external stimulants. But while China's intentions are hard to pin down, its capabilities are easier to measure. They remain limited. The PLA Navy would be hard-pressed to dispatch naval combatants as far as the Straits of Malacca, and it could not long sustain such a deployment.

Despite the advances noted above, the PLA confronts many obstacles:

- The sophistication of new equipment generally exceeds current joint command-and-control capabilities.

- Its reliance on a blend of obsolete and modern equipment makes effective large-scale planning, training, and operations difficult.

- Its dependence on multiple foreign arms suppliers makes it hard to build efficient supply chains and maintenance regimes.

- It has a shortage of technically knowledgeable, innovative, initiative-taking personnel who can operate high-tech systems, a deficiency exacerbated by China's lack of a professional corps of noncommissioned officers.

- It has little combat experience—Chinese military forces have not been involved in major combat since 1979, when they performed poorly against Vietnamese forces.

- It lacks many of the instruments of force projection, including long-range bombers, aircraft carriers, large airborne units, and the logistics capability to support and sustain combat forces beyond its borders.

None of these obstacles can be overcome swiftly, and none can be overcome merely by throwing more money at the problem.

PLA Rivals Also Modernizing

Even as China has been modernizing its armed forces, some of its neighbors and potential adversaries—Japan, South Korea, and Russia— have not been dormant. Despite the fact that it spends less than 1 percent of GDP on defense, Japan has significantly upgraded capabilities over the past fifteen years, deploying the Aegis radar system and accompanying missile systems for its navy and advanced fighter aircraft armed with advanced air-to-air missiles for its air force. Japan is working in partnership with the United States to develop theater missile defenses, primarily oriented against the North Korean threat, but with obvious application in the event of any conflict with China. Since 2002, Japan has sustained a naval presence in the Indian Ocean in support of Operation Enduring Freedom in Afghanistan—in the process gaining valuable experience in operations far from Japanese bases. South Korea has also undertaken a major modernization drive, replacing antiquated fighter aircraft, frigates, tanks, and artillery pieces with advanced systems, many of them purchased from the United States or developed in partnership with U.S. defense industries. South Korean forces enjoy a high level of interoperability with U.S. forces, proven again during South Korea's deployment of more than three thousand troops to Iraq.

Russia is simultaneously China's largest supplier of advanced military hardware and also a potential great power rival. Russia experienced a significant decline in its overall military capabilities during the 1990s, but buoyed by strong oil revenues, Moscow seems poised to begin a significant force modernization drive. Russia's official defense budget has nearly quadrupled from $8.1 billion in 2001 to more than $31 billion in 2006. Russia's defense minister announced an ambitious eight-year, $190 billion modernization plan in February 2007. The plan calls for the replacement of roughly 45 percent of existing equipment, including the deployment of dozens of advanced IBCMs, thirty-one new naval vessels (including eight ballistic missile submarines), and the possibility of a new aircraft carrier. Although Russia may not complete all of these ambitious plans, Moscow's growing capabilities will complicate China's defense planning and force posture as it keeps a wary eye on its 4,300-km border with Russia.

Given the relatively high priority China attaches to Taiwan in its military modernization, Taiwan's own force modernization efforts are most relevant when evaluating China's growing capabilities. During the 1990s, Taiwan acquired 150 F-16s and 60 Mirage advanced fighter aircraft, frigates, surface-to-air missiles, and airborne early warning aircraft from the United States and France. Taiwan also worked to develop indigenous cruise missiles, surface-to-air missiles, and fighter aircraft systems, trying to sustain a qualitative edge over the more numerous Chinese forces. But more recently, Taiwan's defense spending has actually *decreased*. The government of Taiwan has failed to appropriate funds to purchase $18 billion in arms authorized for sale to the island by

President Bush in 2001, a package including submarines, antisubmarine patrol aircraft, and missile defense systems. Taiwan is pursuing a $3 billion purchase of sixty new F-16 fighter aircraft to offset the retirement of aging F-5 fighters. But funding for this purchase has not yet been appropriated, and the United States is urging Taiwan to resolve at least some of the outstanding arms procurement issues before making any new requests.

For its part, the United States is upgrading forward deployed naval and air forces in the Pacific theater (especially on Guam), and will for the first time base a nuclear-powered aircraft carrier in Japan. The United States is improving interoperability with its major Asian allies, staging more realistic and complex multilateral training exercises. The United States is also expanding military cooperation with India, Mongolia, and Indonesia. American air and maritime forces are one to three generations ahead of China's, while U.S. defense spending is about eight times that of China. U.S. forces have significant recent large-scale combat experience and have mastered joint, integrated operations. The United States continues to dominate the region's sealanes, through which flow much of the oil and other commodities on which China's economy depend. Finally, China's defense planning is complicated by the U.S. troop presence in Central Asia, to say nothing of China's long borders with Russia and India, both of which maintain large, modern armed forces.

The Task Force finds that many of China's neighbors and potential adversaries are closely marking China's military modernization and making adjustments to their own defense plans and expenditures that help to balance China's growing military capabilities. But Taiwan has failed to keep pace with China's defense modernization, shifting more of the burden to deter potential Chinese military action onto the United States.

The Bottom Line on China's Military Modernization

Evaluations of military balance must go beyond side-by-side numerical comparisons. They require assessments of the potential military missions of the country. China's principal military missions include deterring a nuclear attack, defending its territory in depth, dissuading Taiwan from steps toward independence, and, if necessary, attacking Taiwan or even taking it by force. In the future, China could expand the mission of the PLA, defending more far-flung interests. So far, China has taken only modest steps in this direction, participating in multilateral peacekeeping missions as far away as Africa. The military missions of the United States in East Asia both for the present and the future are to protect its friends and allies from aggression, to defeat those who use terrorism, to prevent nuclear proliferation, and more generally to provide a stable security environment within which the nations of the region can enjoy peace and prosperity.

The principal area in which the mission sets of the United States and China currently come into potential conflict is Taiwan. China can damage Taiwan with missiles, but it can only take and hold Taiwan if it can win and sustain control of the space, air, and waters around Taiwan—a difficult task without U.S. intervention, and nearly impossible should the United States intervene in a China-Taiwan war.

The Task Force finds that as a consequence of its military modernization, China is making progress toward being able to fight and win a war with Taiwan (absent U.S. intervention), and it is also beginning to build capabilities to safeguard its growing global interests. The mere existence of these capabilities—including anti-satellite systems—poses challenges for the United States. China does not need to surpass the United States, or even catch up with the United States, in order to complicate U.S. defense planning or influence U.S. decision-making in the event of a crisis in the Taiwan Strait or elsewhere. *Looking ahead as far as 2030, however, the Task Force finds no evidence to support the notion that China will become a peer military competitor of the United States. By virtue of its heritage and experience, its equipment and level of technology, its personnel, and the resources it spends, the United States enjoys space, air, and naval superiority over China. The military balance today and for the foreseeable future strongly favors the United States and its allies.*

U.S.-China Relations

The preceding pages analyzed recent trends in China's economic and social transformation, its foreign policies, and its military modernization. The complex picture that emerges underscores a central observation about China in the American political arena: It is not unusual for assessments of China within the U.S. government or even within one administration to differ, sometimes radically. China defies easy definition. And different parts of the U.S. government often prioritize U.S. interests with China differently, leading some officials to see and note progress while others witness none. In 2002, the Bush administration's national security strategy report stressed that the United States had "profound" disagreements with China over Taiwan and human rights, condemned China for its failure to embrace democracy and freedom of religion, and took a particularly dim view of China's defense modernization, warning, "In pursuing advanced military capabilities that can threaten its neighbors in the Asia-Pacific region, China is following an outdated path that, in the end, will hamper its own pursuit of national greatness. In time, China will find that social and political freedom is the only source of that greatness."[36] Two years later, in 2004, then Secretary of State Colin Powell declared that U.S.-China relations were in the best shape since the Nixon-Mao rapprochement of 1972.[37] Three years later, in February 2007, Vice President Dick Cheney pointedly reiterated the administration's deep concerns about

---

[36] The National Security Strategy of the United States of America, September 2002, p. 27.
[37] "Powell: China Ties Best in 30 Years," *The China Daily News*, November 11, 2004.

China's military modernization, stating China's "fast-paced military buildup" was "not consistent with China's stated goal of a 'peaceful rise.'"[38]

Such divergent public views of China reflect both contending policy views within the administration and the diversity of China itself. However they detract from the effectiveness of U.S. policy toward China. *The Task Force finds that the United States must pursue a consistent policy to integrate China into the global community with the goal of building on areas where interests converge (or potentially converge) and narrowing areas of differences. For the long term, U.S. policy must make allowances for the uncertainties in China's future development. And even in the short term, the United States must stand ready to challenge China when its conduct is at odds with U.S. vital interests, using all the elements of its national power—adherence to its ideals of human rights, the rule of law and representative government, diplomatic power and influence, economic strength and dynamism, and military capabilities.*

Against this backdrop, the Task Force now turns to a more detailed look at specific elements of U.S.-China relations.

Economic Relations

In his "stakeholder" speech, then Deputy Secretary of State Zoellick correctly pointed out that U.S.-China relations are threatened by China's failure to stop the theft of U.S. intellectual property and the undervaluation of China's currency, both of which contribute to the U.S. trade deficit with China. Indeed, concerns about these and other unfair trade practices have great potential to roil the U.S.-China relationship, particularly given the strong reaction these issues generate in the U.S. Congress. The United States has been a prime driver of the process of economic globalization, but support for globalization is predicated on the notion that all nations will play by the rules. The perception that China is breaking the rules, or at least exploiting ambiguities in the system in ways that disadvantage the United States, undermines

---

[38] Vice President's Remarks to the Australian-American Leadership Dialogue, speech delivered on February 23, 2007, available at http://www.whitehouse.gov/news/releases/2007/02/20070223.html.

support not only for cooperative U.S.-China relations specifically, but economic globalization more generally.

IPR Concerns

A study by the U.S. Chamber of Commerce estimates that intellectual property rights (IPR) violations cost U.S. firms between $200 billion and $250 billion a year globally, with a significant portion of that attributed to Chinese piracy. Commerce Secretary Carlos M. Gutierrez estimates that Chinese piracy of digital media (CDs and DVDs) alone costs U.S. firms about $2.3 billion each year. The Task Force finds these numbers significantly overestimate the actual damage, as they assume that consumers of cheap pirated products would buy the same volume of U.S. products if the pirated versions were unavailable. In fact, Chinese demand is elastic, and many Chinese consumers do not have sufficient income to buy the higher-priced genuine items. None-theless, the fact remains that it is easy to walk down any shopping avenue in China or even into brand-name department stores and detect fake merchandise. It is much harder, however, to find a pirated version of the mascot for the Beijing Olympics.

Efforts to get China to improve IPR protection go back to the early 1990s when China and the United States negotiated a series of bilateral agreements requiring China to enact laws to protect intellectual property from patents to copyright. In March 2007, China acceded to the World Intellectual Property Organization (WIPO) Copyright Treaty and the WIPO Performances and Phonograms Treaty, the two treaties that comprise the WIPO Internet Treaties. Increasingly, China has the laws, but two problems remain: enforcement and punishment. Some high-profile actions have protected trademarks for Pfizer, General Motors, Starbucks, and Kodak, but enforcement remains spotty and U.S. leverage has not been strong. There are no WTO-established metrics for determining what constitutes effective enforcement, and no country is required to make IPR enforcement a higher priority than other areas of law enforcement. A case brought against China on the grounds that its laws and regulations fail to meet WTO standards would likely fail because China's laws and regulations in fact meet WTO requirements. Moreover, American firms, fearing loss of business, have been reluctant to provide detailed information to the government to bring a case before the WTO. A second difficulty involves punishment. The penalties provided by China's IPR law are modest, so even when there is enforcement, the deterrent effect is minimal.

In the long run, China's willingness to enhance protection of intellectual property will increase as it sees the intellectual property of its own firms threatened by lax enforcement. This is beginning to happen. According to China's State Administration for Industry and Commerce (SAIC), applications by Chinese firms to register trademarks and file patents have soared in recent years. With the increase in Chinese applications has come an increase in investigations and litigation involving alleged infringement, most of which involve Chinese complainants.

The Task Force finds that China has failed to adequately protect American intellectual property, a failure that has as much to do with a lack of will as it does with a lack of capability. The rampant theft of intellectual property rights is undermining support for closer U.S.-China economic relations in the U.S. business community and in Congress. To date, Chinese efforts to address U.S. IPR concerns have been sorely inadequate.

Currency Values

The undervaluation of China's currency is another major cause of friction between the United States and China. There is little question that the Chinese currency is undervalued, contributing modestly to the U.S. trade deficit with China. But there is considerable doubt about whether a rapid, major appreciation of the yuan would prove beneficial to the United States. As discussed below, the value of the yuan is not a major cause of the U.S. trade deficit with China, and the United States should not expect appreciation of the yuan to resolve its trade difficulties with China.

China's current account surplus grew from about 2 percent of GDP in 2002 to over 6 percent of GDP in 2005, and is continuing to climb. In each of the past three years, China's foreign exchange market intervention has been massive, averaging about $200 billion per year. As a result of these interventions, China surpassed Japan to become the world's largest single holder of foreign exchange reserves early in 2006, amassing more than $1 trillion in reserves.

Given these facts, why does China keep the value of its currency artificially low? Monetary policy necessarily involves an internal policy debate in China. China's leaders are concerned that any dramatic move to increase the value of the yuan would harm China's economy in three ways: (1) by sucking in food imports and thereby depressing agricultural earnings; (2) by reducing exports and export-linked job creation; and (3) by jeopardizing the credit extended to support China's excessive investment in recent years in mostly state-owned heavy industries (steel, cement, chemicals). An appreciation of the yuan could put in jeopardy many of these loans that were extended not on the basis of creditworthiness, but on the basis of political pressures, which would in turn put greater strain on China's fragile banking system.

Notwithstanding these concerns, Beijing is moving slowly to adjust the value of the yuan. The framework for a more flexible exchange rate by China was established in midsummer 2005. China began by increasing the value of the yuan against the dollar 2.1 percent. Subsequent adjustments are limited to a daily correction of 0.03 percent. Overall, the value of the yuan has risen about 6.5 percent against the dollar since the more flexible exchange rate policy was implemented in 2005.

Members of Congress frustrated by China's currency policy introduced legislation in 2005 designed to compel China to allow the yuan to appreciate. The Schumer-Graham bill, which enjoyed broad bipartisan support in the Senate, called for across-the-board 27 percent tariffs on Chinese exports to the United States unless China adjusted its currency to reflect market rates. Under pressure from the Bush administration and after visiting China in the summer of 2006, Senators Schumer and Graham withdrew their bill in the fall of 2006. But they pledged to reintroduce a similar measure in the new Congress. Meanwhile, Senate Finance Committee Chairman Max Baucus (D-MN) and Ranking Member Charles Grassley (R-IA) have expressed interest in introducing their own bill, designed to be compliant with the WTO, to address concerns about the value of the yuan.

What would happen if China were to allow its currency to appreciate significantly against the dollar—by 25 percent or more? The result would depend heavily on the movements of other Asian currencies, since roughly 65 percent of the value of China's exports to the United States is accounted for by Chinese imports from other countries of components, parts, and raw materials. If other Asian nations don't allow their currencies to rise, then the cost of China's imports from their Asian neighbors would fall in terms of the yuan and the increase in China's export prices would be quite modest. Price moves would probably reduce the U.S.-China trade imbalance somewhat, perhaps by $20 billion to $40 billion, although experts differ on the impact. In the past eighteen months, although the value of the yuan has risen 6.5 percent against the dollar, Chinese exports to the United States and the U.S. trade deficit with China have actually *grown*, not shrunk.

But if other Asian nations allowed their currencies to rise with a significant appreciation of the yuan, the effect on the U.S. global current account deficit would be much greater. Not only would the yuan price of China's imports rise—increasing the price of Chinese goods on the global market—but the price of other Asian exports to the United States would also rise. Such a coordinated move of Asian currencies could have a significant impact on the U.S. current account deficit, several times the $20 billion to $40 billion estimate above.

But a major revaluation of the yuan could also have *negative* side effects for both the United States and China. A weakening of the dollar against the yuan could result in higher U.S. interest rates if China sells devalued Treasuries—undermining the U.S. housing sector—and it could also spark instability in China's banking sector. The Chinese economy could slow, with a corresponding impact on the economies of its East Asian trading partners, especially Japan, and on the U.S. economy. Alternatively, armed with a more valuable yuan, Chinese firms might go on a shopping expedition in the United States, reinforcing, rather than relaxing, economic anxieties. As one columnist put it, "If you think China is big news in Washington today, just wait until companies in the world's fourth biggest economy start bidding for General Motors, Microsoft, Boeing or Exxon-Mobil."[39]

The value of the yuan is inseparable from one of the underlying causes of the U.S. trade deficit with China: patterns of consumption

---

[39] William Pesek, "For U.S., China Isn't the Problem," *International Herald Tribune*, December 14, 2006.

and savings. In short, the United States consumes too much and saves too little, and China does the opposite. Household consumption in China as a share of GDP has been falling since 2000, and by 2005 accounted for 38 percent of GDP, down from an average of 46 percent in the 1990s.[40] Chinese are saving more in large measure because they are responsible for more aspects of their lives than ever before, and must now pay for housing, health care, and retirement. In 2004, China announced plans to shift from an investment- and export-driven model of development toward a consumption-led growth path.[41] But so far, the results have been meager, and China's external surplus continues to mushroom. China's efforts to move toward a consumption-led growth model would be enhanced by government noninvestment expenditures on health care, education, welfare, and pensions—expenditures that would not only fuel consumer demand but also free up private resources for consumption.

The Task Force finds that attempts to pressure China into raising the value of its currency by threatening tariffs are well intentioned but misguided, and could well backfire. A change in relative currency values has to be part of any policy package that significantly reduces the U.S. trade deficit with China, but focusing so much congressional attention and political prestige on the issue is a misapplication of resources that could be better applied elsewhere. Changing patterns of U.S and Chinese consumption and the fact that China has become the final stop in Asia's supply chain of products for the shelves of U.S. retailers are among the factors driving the trade imbalance. The trade deficit with China will shrink if the United States and China rectify their own macroeconomic policies. For China, this means emphasizing consumption-led growth and spending more on social services like health care and social security. China also needs to shore up its banking system and capital markets. The United States has an interest in helping China improve the regulation and monitoring of the soundness of its

---

[40] Nicholas R. Lardy, "China: Toward a Consumption-Driven Growth Path," Institute for International Economics Policy Brief, October 2006, available at http://www.petersoninstitute.org/publications. The China consumption rate is the lowest of any major economy in the world. In the United States, consumption accounted for 70 percent of GDP in 2005, and in India it was 61 percent.

[41] "Central Economic Work Conference Convenes in Beijing December 3 to 5," *People's Daily*, December 6, 2004.

capital markets, as a robust internal capital market will help reduce China's overdependence on tremendous capital inflows that it cannot absorb efficiently.

Benefits and Fairness

A growing number of Americans believe that trade with China harms the U.S. economy and that the U.S. trade deficit with China is mainly the result of unfair Chinese trade practices. Both notions are false. But that does not mean that competition with China is always benign or fair. Certain sectors of the U.S. economy have been hurt by Chinese competition, and according to the U.S. trade representative, some of China's economic policies constitute an unfair subsidy of exports in violation of China's WTO obligations.[42]

A recent study found that U.S. prices will be 0.8 percent lower and U.S. GDP will be 0.7 percent higher in 2010 as a result of increased bilateral trade and investment in China since 2001. This translates into an increase of $1,000 in disposable income per average household per year.[43] A joint IIE-CSIS study concluded that the U.S. economy as a whole was roughly $70 billion richer as a result of trade with China, and that "the overall [economic] impact should be a continuing, increasing, positive boost to output, productivity, employment, and real wages." Another comprehensive study of U.S.-China economic relations, this one completed recently by the Congressional Research Service, concluded, "China's economic ascendancy will not in and of itself undermine or lower U.S. living standards—these will be largely determined by U.S. economic policies. . . Thus far the overall impact of China's economic growth and opening up to the world appears to have been positive for both the U.S. and Chinese economies."[44]

---

[42] See http://usinfo.state.gov/xarchives/display.html?P = washfile-english&y = 2007& m = March&x = 20070312144030zjsredna0.2189752.

[43] Oxford Economics and the Signal Group, "The China Effect: Assessing the Impact on the U.S. Economy of Trade and Investment with China," The China Business Forum, January 2006, p. 17.

[44] Craig K. Elwell, Marc Labonte, and Wayne M. Morrison, "Is China a Threat to the U.S. Economy?" Congressional Research Service, January 23, 2007, available at http:// www.fas.org/sgp/crs/row/RL33604.pdf.

Because U.S. savings are insufficient to finance total spending and investment, America must borrow from abroad, and that results in much of the world, including China, running a current account surplus with the United States. Far from being closed to U.S. exports, China is actually the fastest-growing export market for the United States and China ranks among the most open of all developing economies. Between 2000 and 2005, U.S. exports to China grew by some 160 percent, while exports to the rest of the world grew only 10 percent. China accounted for half the growth of exports of U.S. firms in this five-year period. Two-way trade grew from $990 million in 1978 to $285 billion in 2005. China is now the United States' third-largest trading partner while the United States is China's largest trading partner. China's applied tariffs on imports are low, its use of quotas is limited to tariff rate quotas for a few agricultural products, and it has eliminated licensing requirements for imports largely on schedule with its WTO commitments. China's ratio of imports to GDP is half again as high as that of India (where applied tariffs are almost three times China's), twice that of the United States, and three times Japan's.

Moreover, most of what Americans buy from China today was once purchased from other East Asian countries. The share of the overall U.S. trade deficit accounted for by East Asia taken as a whole has in fact *declined* from just over half in 1985 (when China's share of that deficit was zero) to 40 percent in 2004 (when China's share was 25 percent). Producers throughout East Asia, particularly those from Hong Kong, Japan, Singapore, South Korea, and Taiwan, have moved a substantial portion of their production capacity to China. The U.S. trade deficit with China has increased in parallel with the increase of foreign investment (mostly Asian) in production facilities in China.[45]

China has an extremely open environment for foreign investment and since economic reforms began in 1978 has attracted more than

---

[45] The correlation is striking. In the early 1980s, the FDI inflows into China were about $500 million per year, foreign firms' exports from China accounted for less than 1 percent of the total, and the United States had a significant surplus in its trade with China. By the mid-1990s, investment inflows to China rose to about $45 billion per year, foreign firms accounted for one-third of China's exports, and the U.S. bilateral deficit with China jumped to about $30 billion. In 2005, China attracted roughly $60 billion in FDI. That year, foreign firms (mostly Asian) made about 65 percent of the goods that the United States imported from China, and the U.S. bilateral deficit with China shot to over $200 billion.

$600 billion in foreign direct investment, about two-thirds of which has gone into manufacturing. More than three-quarters of this FDI originates from countries throughout Asia. Foreign firms located in China now produce almost 30 percent of China's manufactured goods, slightly ahead of the share of foreign firms in the production of manufactured goods in the EU, half again as high as the share in the United States, and about twenty-five times that in Japan.

The Task Force finds that on balance, U.S. trade relations with China benefit the people of the United States as well as China. The large bilateral trade deficit with China is part of a global trend: not unique to China, and not essentially attributable to Chinese restrictions on market access, low Chinese wage rates, or other discriminatory trade practices. Yet China has not yet brought all of its economic policies into compliance with its WTO obligations, making concerted U.S. action desirable both to protect U.S. workers from unfair competition and to bolster the legitimacy of the overall global trading system.

This brings us to the final major concern about China's economic competition with the United States: jobs.

American Jobs

Many Americans understandably associate their own job insecurity with economic growth in the developing world, especially China. The loss of manufacturing jobs in the United States is a particular concern, but the issue of outsourcing has such political traction because white-collar jobs (legal services, accounting, medical services) are also migrating overseas.

Manufacturing's share of U.S. employment has been declining ever since the end of World War II. The growth of productivity has outstripped the growth in demand, as consumers have devoted an ever-larger share of their spending to services instead of goods.[46] From 2000 to 2003, manufacturing experienced a sharp decline in employment, shedding 2.85 million jobs. These losses coincided with steady increases in the U.S. trade deficit with China, leading some observers to see causality.

---

[46] For a detailed examination of the loss of U.S. manufacturing jobs, see David Brauer, "What Accounts for the Decline in Manufacturing Employment?" U.S. Congressional Budget Office, February 18, 2004.

In fact, the growth in imported manufactured goods was sluggish during this period (about 2 percent), and a study by McKinsey & Company found that global trade accounted for only 314,000 of the 2.85 million lost manufacturing jobs. Another study by the Economic Policy Institute using the same raw data but different methodology found that roughly six hundred thousand lost jobs can be attributed to the impact of foreign trade. The other jobs disappeared because of productivity increases, the economy's cyclical downturn, and a slump in exports. Even using the higher estimate for total manufacturing job losses attributable to trade—six hundred thousand—China's impact would be modest since China accounted for only 25 percent of the U.S. trade deficit from 2000 to 2003.

Outsourcing—particularly moving production to China to then export products back to the U.S. market—is also often blamed for U.S. job losses. But according to a Governement Accountability Office (GAO) report, beginning in 2002, sales of goods to China by U.S. affiliates there grew faster than—and exceeded—U.S. exports to China, suggesting that most U.S. firms were using their investments in China to access the Chinese market, rather than using China-based production to sell to the U.S. market.[47]

Such studies run up against a stubborn political reality: The pain associated with job losses is acute and localized while the benefits to the overall economy are often diffuse and rarely attributed to economic relations with China. More than a third of all recent manufacturing job losses are concentrated in seven Great Lakes states: Illinois, Indiana, Michigan, New York, Ohio, Pennsylvania, and Wisconsin. And while some of these job losses have been offset by new service sector employment created by foreign trade, many of those service sector jobs may not be available to workers from manufacturing plants, and in any event, the service sector jobs are in most cases not equal to the manufacturing jobs in salary and benefits.

The Task Force finds that the growth of U.S.-China economic relations is occurring against the backdrop of a shift in the structure of U.S. employment from manufacturing to services. China is by no means the only cause of this

---

[47] "China Trade: U.S. Exports, Investment, Affiliate Sales Rising but Export Share Falling," GAO-06-162, December 2005, p. 35.

transition, nor is it a major source of U.S. job loss. An effective U.S. response to this shift in employment, therefore, requires not only encouraging China to play by the rules of international trade, but more importantly making sure the American workforce is as educated and trained as humanly possible, and that policies are in place to ensure workers against sudden job loss—unemployment insurance, health care portability, retraining programs, etc.

U.S.-China Security Relations

While economic links between the United States and China are robust and growing, military-to-military relations remain relatively undeveloped, even though tough problems, such as North Korea's nuclear ambitions, require close coordination. Chairman of the Joint Chiefs of Staff Marine General Peter Pace, while visiting China in March 2007, called for closer security ties to "avoid misunderstandings and help build greater stability and prosperity in Asia."[48]

Soon after he took office, President Bush put the military-to-military relationship on hold while the administration conducted a China policy review. Relations reached a low point in the spring of 2001 when a Chinese naval aviation F-8 fighter plane intercepted a U.S. EP-3 electronic surveillance aircraft operating off the coast of Hainan Island in international airspace. The Chinese fighter aircraft shadowed the EP-3 and eventually collided with the slow-moving reconnaissance aircraft, resulting in the death of the Chinese pilot and forcing the pilot of the EP-3 to make an emergency landing at a Chinese military airbase on Hainan. The U.S. crew was held for eleven days before being repatriated. Acrimony over the incident put military ties on hold indefinitely. The EP-3 incident became a metaphor for U.S.-China military relations, just as Tiananmen has come to symbolize the Chinese government's resistance to political reforms.

After this rocky start, bilateral military interactions have rebounded in recent years, particularly since 9/11, and now include a program of high-level dialogue, working-level talks, reciprocal ship visits, and

---

[48] Jim Garamone, "Pace Visit Paves Way for Better Relations with China," available at http://www.defenselink.mil/news/newsarticle.aspx?id=32579.

functional exchanges. In 2005, Secretary of Defense Donald H. Rumsfeld visited China for the first time in his tenure and, during the visit, was the first known foreigner to be given a tour of the headquarters of China's strategic missile forces, the Second Artillery. In 2006, the U.S. and Chinese Navy conducted two exercises: a passing exercise (PASSEX) and a search-and-rescue exercise (SAREX) near Hawaii. These events were a significant breakthrough and included the first visit by Chinese naval vessels to a U.S. port since 2000.

Yet military relations remain modest and are hampered by mistrust. Washington and Beijing have had difficulty talking about two issues at the heart of the bilateral military relationship: Taiwan and strategic nuclear forces. President Bush and President Hu agreed in April 2006 to several confidence-building measures, including opening a dialogue on China's strategic forces modernization and U.S. national missile defenses, but little has been accomplished to date.

Improving communication requires tackling the twin issues of reciprocity and transparency in bilateral military interactions. Beijing has resisted efforts by the Department of Defense to achieve greater military transparency in the bilateral relationship, arguing, "transparency is a tool of the strong to be used against the weak." The latest Chinese defense white paper, a biannual publication, is a step in the right direction, but is of limited use given the general data in it. Greater transparency would enable each side to better understand the other's doctrine and capabilities.

The Task Force finds that a sustained and systematic official dialogue on military affairs would enhance trust and reduce the potential for miscommunication and miscalculation, particularly during crisis periods. In order to convince China to be more open about its defense plans, the United States will have to be more open about its own. But even then, China is unlikely to provide full reciprocity. This should not dissuade the United States from engaging with the PLA, as more robust exchanges would expose the PLA to outside perspectives and also ensure that China accurately comprehends the degree to which the military balance today and for the foreseeable future favors the United States.

North Korea and the Six-Party Talks

The current efforts to deal with North Korea are the most significant cooperative security activity among Northeast Asian states. If the talks succeed, they could lay the foundation for a new multilateral security mechanism for Northeast Asia, and for further security cooperation among the United States, China, Russia, Japan, South Korea, and North Korea in other areas. *But if despite recent progress, the talks ultimately fail, U.S.-China security relations could become more strained if the two nations diverge over what to do next about the North's nuclear programs.*

China and the United States view the challenges posed by North Korea differently. Both nations share an interest in promoting economic reforms in the North. Beijing has been encouraging the economic opening of North Korea for years, training Democratic People's Republic of Korea (DPRK) economists, showcasing the achievements of the Chinese economic development strategy, and trying to pull North Korea out of its shell. China's leaders resent having to support the economically bankrupt North Korean state. They do not get along with Kim Jong-Il, and the comradeship that used to bond the People's Liberation Army to the Korean People's Army is a thing of the past.

But China and the United States have divergent views on the threats posed by North Korea. Chinese leaders are acutely concerned about a crumbling North Korea that precipitates massive instability in northeastern China, exacerbating tensions in an already volatile part of the country. This is a national security concern for China. China feels only an indirect nuclear threat from the North: It doubts seriously that North Korea would ever use or export a nuclear device given the devastation this would bring down on North Korea's head. But China does take seriously the destabilizing effects of the North's nuclear program and seeks its total abolition, especially because of its side effects. Specifically, China worries that the United States might take military action against North Korea (causing refugee flows and chaos), that the United States might lead a drive for international sanctions on the North designed to cripple or even topple the regime (forcing China to "choose sides"), or that Japan might choose to develop nuclear weapons (undermining an important pillar of China's global security strategy and perhaps encouraging South Korea and even Taiwan to revisit their nuclear options).

The effort to balance these various considerations helps explain Beijing's reluctance to apply maximum pressure on the North Korean regime, even though it is willing to use some of its considerable leverage. China provides roughly 90 percent of North Korea's oil, an important input not only for power generation but also for the North Korean military. And although North Korea generates more than 80 percent of its electric power using indigenous coal, an oil cutoff would severely crimp North Korea's economy and strain the Korean People's Army.

China also opposes steps that might back North Korea into a corner because it is worried about how Kim Jong-Il would behave in a crisis, and it doubts whether any North Korean government that might succeed him would be an improvement on the Kim dynasty. A final factor contributing to China's reticence to use all of its leverage is its lingering doubts about the strategic intentions of the United States. Does the United States seek a denuclearized Korean Peninsula, or regime change in North Korea? Both? Does the United States seek a unified, nuclear Korea, with U.S. forces stationed there?

In contrast with China, The United States views North Korea's possession of nuclear weapons as a *direct* threat to the United States and its allies, the Republic of Korea and Japan. Moreover, Washington has a long-standing commitment to global nonproliferation efforts, and the United States—especially post-9/11—has profound concerns about the potential North Korean export of nuclear materials. The United States does not trust North Korea to safeguard such materials.

North Korea's actions in recent months—firing a barrage of missiles in July 2006, exploding a nuclear device in October 2006, and then finally reiterating in principle on February 13, 2007, its agreement to abandon its nuclear programs in exchange for a package of economic and political incentives—provide an opportunity for the United States and China to narrow their differences and better align their strategic objectives and policies. China's backing for UN sanctions on North Korea suggests a newfound willingness to contemplate coercive measures against the North to complement traditional Chinese offers of reassurance to Pyongyang. And the United States' willingness to engage in direct bilateral talks with North Korea to complement the Six Party Talks suggests a new spirit of flexibility and a rejection of regime change as a realistic option for U.S. policy. The United States might be able to coax even more cooperation out of Beijing if it launched a dialogue with Beijing exploring each nation's long-term interests and goals on the Korean Peninsula.

The Task Force finds that despite differing threat perceptions of North Korea, the United States and China have an opportunity to expand areas of policy coordination and, in concert with Japan and especially South Korea, to begin to form a common vision for the future of the Korean Peninsula. A more balanced blend of incentives and disincentives—"Asian sticks" and "American carrots" to go along with the "Asian carrots" and "American sticks"—could yield positive results and maximize the chance that North Korea will follow through on its commitments of September 19, 2005, and February 13, 2007, to denuclearize.

Export Controls and Sanctions on Technology Transfer

China's economic and military modernization efforts rely heavily on technologies acquired from abroad, although as discussed above, that dependence is gradually shrinking as China builds up its own technological base. Until the Tiananmen tragedy, the United States actively encouraged and facilitated China's acquisition of many advanced technologies, even those with direct military applications, to bolster China as a counterweight to Soviet power. Although technology exports to China were regulated under the Coordinating Committee for Multilateral Export Controls regime (COCOM), China generally received much more favorable treatment than did the Soviet Union. Until 1989, China acquired U.S. military hardware through foreign military sales, and also aggressively sought out advanced dual-use technologies such as machine tools, computers, and aerospace systems.

It was not until after Tiananmen and the collapse of the Soviet Union that U.S. attitudes about technology transfer to China changed, and abruptly. Technology transfer became a point of leverage over China, and new laws attempted to use that leverage to modify Chinese foreign and domestic policies. Congress and the George H.W. Bush administration banned the sale of military hardware to China after Tiananmen, requiring improvements in China's human rights policies before sales could resume. Congress restricted nuclear cooperation, strictly linking it to cooperation on U.S. nonproliferation goals. Congress similarly imposed sanctions on space cooperation—including the launch of U.S. satellites on Chinese rockets—in response to China's proliferation of missile technology.[49]

The Department of Commerce is currently considering restrictions on forty-seven new categories of dual-use technologies. Business associations find the new regulations confusing and point out that for most, if not all, of the technologies on the proposed list, there is a producer in the European Union, Japan, or China itself. This means that to be effective, any export controls would have to be multilateral. This will not be easy to accomplish. In 2005, the United States had to work hard to convince the EU to sustain its prohibition on arms sales to China (a restriction in place since Tiananmen). This transatlantic dialogue succeeded in sensitizing many EU policymakers to U.S. security interests in Asia as well as the rapid pace and scope of PLA modernization. With the possible exception of France, there currently do not appear to be any strong forces within the EU advocating abolishment of the arms embargo. For the most part, however, the members of the EU want to expand, not restrict, technology exports to China, hoping to gain an ever-larger share of the growing Chinese technology market. U.S. consultations with Japan suggest a similar dynamic is under way in Tokyo, particularly given Prime Minister Abe's desire to continue the recent thaw in Sino-Japanese relations. One result of the EU and U.S. arms embargo has been to encourage China to develop a robust arms supply relationship with Russia, involving purchases, coproduction, training, and joint maneuvers.

The Department of Commerce also recently proposed, and then withdrew, new restrictions on "deemed exports." These new regulations would have made it more difficult for American companies and universities to hire Chinese (and other foreign students) to work in laboratories. After a massive outcry from business associations and universities—which argued that if the United States was worried about competitiveness and its ability to train and attract the best and the brightest it ought not to treat these students as second-class citizens— the proposal was withdrawn. But new proposals are being considered.

---

[49] This stands in marked contrast with the Reagan era, when the United States chose to launch satellites on Chinese rockets after the space shuttle *Challenger* disaster even though China was actively selling arms to Iran at the time.

China has complained that U.S. restrictions on high-technology exports contribute significantly to the U.S.-China trade deficit. *The Task Force finds this argument unconvincing and empirically false.* There are legitimate national security and economic security reasons for the United States to restrict some sensitive technologies to China, including the risk that such technologies—even if not employed by China against U.S. interests—might fall into the hands of those who mean to do harm to the United States. Export licensing stopped only about 1.5 percent of the value of exports to China in 2005. Out of $39 billion in U.S. exports, only about $3 billion worth even required export licenses from the Commerce Department, and almost all of those exports were eventually approved, according to Commerce Department data.

Today, the United States continues to use export controls and sanctions on technology transfer to protect transfers of sensitive goods, punish China for actions contrary to U.S. interests (such as proliferation), or to create incentives for China to change its foreign or domestic policies. The Bush administration has sanctioned dozens of Chinese firms for violating U.S. export controls regulations, often for selling dual-use technologies to Iran, Libya, or North Korea.

The Task Force finds that the selective application of sanctions on technology flow can sometimes shape China's conduct in the realm of foreign affairs— particularly when the sanctions are accompanied by concerted high-profile public diplomacy, as was the case with Silkworm cruise missile exports to Iran. Sanctions are less likely to convince China to modify its domestic policies. Sanctions are most likely to change China's behavior—by adjusting calculations of China's self-interest—when they curtail China's access to high-value technologies with few alternative suppliers.

Recommendations

Setting the Course

Enhancing U.S.-China cooperation on regional and global challenges begins with a clear statement of U.S. policy goals and priorities communicated not only to Beijing, but also to the American people. Successive administrations have discovered that strong presidential leadership is essential to building a bipartisan consensus among Americans and their elected representatives in support of pursuing a close and cooperative relationship with China. China policy is set by the president, but also influenced by Congress and by the many departments and agencies of the U.S. government charged with implementing policy. As the 110th Congress works under new leadership, and as the Bush administration completes its final months in office, it is an opportune time to discuss how best to enhance U.S.-China cooperation on pressing regional and global challenges and then to forge a policy consensus to carry the nation through the next electoral cycle and into a new administration in 2009.

President Bush provided a clear statement of the overall U.S. approach toward China when he hosted Chinese President Hu Jintao in Washington in April 2006. President Bush said, "The United States and China are two nations divided by a vast ocean—yet connected through a global economy that has created opportunity for both peoples. The United States welcomes the emergence of a China that is peaceful and prosperous, and that supports international institutions. As stake-holders in the international system, the two nations share many strategic

73

interests. President Hu and I will discuss how to advance those interests, and how China and the United States can cooperate responsibly with other nations to address common challenges." The president said later in the same statement that he would candidly raise differences with President Hu: that the United States would not neglect areas of China's foreign and domestic policies that are of concern to the United States.

As previously stated, the Task Force concurs with the "responsible stakeholder" goal for U.S.-China relations. The Task Force believes integration of China into the global community represents the best strategy to encourage China to act in ways consistent with U.S. interests and international norms. Sustaining support for a close, candid, and cooperative relationship can best be achieved by articulating a positive message—a call to realize the potential benefits of working with China on issues such as nuclear nonproliferation and protecting the global environment. At times, the United States will need to communicate to China that irresponsible or aggressive behavior will meet strong opposition and injure China's core national interests. But more often the United States should encourage China in the direction of responsible global citizenship, forging common responses to regional and global challenges through dialogue and mutual respect.

Accordingly, we begin by recommending that the president reinforce recent efforts to put U.S.-China relations on a positive track by:

- Stating clearly and more often that the United States wants to establish a close, candid, constructive, and collaborative relationship with China.

- Explaining to the American public the many benefits that flow from a strong bilateral relationship.

- Stating forthrightly that a peaceful and secure China, one that is accountable to the Chinese people, is in the interests of the United States. Moreover, the United States also has an interest in a *responsible and cooperative* China that is willing to honor international norms and regimes and to share the burden of addressing regional and global issues in cooperation with others; in a *prosperous and open* China, that serves as an engine for the global economy by welcoming imports and investment from abroad; and in a China whose development is *equitable and sustainable*, paying due attention to the needs of the country's less advantaged and limiting the negative impact of development on the local, regional, and global environment.

- The United States should work closely with other nations—particularly Japan and the members of the European Union—to advance these goals.

- The president should frankly acknowledge that mutual suspicions currently burden U.S.-China relations and call on both nations to take steps to deepen mutual understanding and trust.

Identifying Core Interests

From the earliest days of engagement with Washington, Beijing has tried to communicate its core interests—such as Taiwan—and expected Washington to do the same. *The United States should communicate its core interests clearly to Beijing, because China's track record suggests that when it understands that something is vital to the United States, it is more likely to be responsive to American concerns.* The Task Force recommends that the United States concentrate on the following areas:

- Improving economic relations;
- Enhancing security relations: building mutual understanding and cooperation;
- Strengthening nonproliferation efforts;
- Encouraging political reform, rule of law, and respect for human rights; and
- Protecting the global environment and promoting sustainable energy policies.

These core interests are not rank-ordered. All share a degree of urgency—e.g., the risk that North Korea might export nuclear weapons or know-how, and the threat to the planet posed by global warming. All are important to sustaining political support in the United States and China for the overall relationship. All can and should be worked on simultaneously. None of these U.S. objectives is at odds with China's fundamental national interests. In fact, all are consistent with China's long-term successful emergence as a responsible great power. Even the more difficult objectives—promoting greater respect for human rights and political reform—are consistent with China's stated national objectives, including its desire to sustain economic growth, to promote social harmony and equity, to fight corruption, and to lay the groundwork necessary for peaceful reunification with Taiwan. Achieving significant progress on some of these challenges—environmental protection, for instance—will take time. But the Task Force believes that the more daunting the task, the more reason the United States has to intensify its efforts.

Improving Economic Relations

Getting the economic relationship with China in order requires a blend of domestic reforms in the United States as well as in China, bilateral initiatives, and efforts to integrate China more completely into the international economic system. The United States' overarching objective with China is to ensure that macro- and microeconomic reforms continue. Improving China's adherence to its WTO obligations will help drive the reform process inside China, but other steps are needed to put the bilateral economic relationship on a sound footing.

First, managing U.S. economic relations with China cannot be separated from larger economic policy decisions at home. The United States needs to get its own economic house in order by shrinking deficits, raising savings rates, reducing consumption, strengthening primary and secondary education, and investing in technological innovation. The United States cannot excel in today's global "knowledge age" economy when one-third of its high school students fail to graduate.[50] To maintain public support for open trade that contributes significantly to U.S. wealth, the United States will need to implement more effective labor market adjustment programs to help those adversely affected by the

---

[50] Jay P. Greene and Greg Forster, "Public High School Graduation and College Readiness Rates in the United States," Education Working Paper No. 3, the Manhattan Institute, September 2003.

rapid changes occurring as a result of globalization.[51] Finally, the United States should safeguard U.S. security interests without throwing up barriers to Chinese or other foreign investment. The United States cannot credibly argue for open investment policies abroad if it imposes or threatens to impose additional hurdles for foreign acquisitions of U.S. companies that raise no security threat, as it did when China National Offshore Oil Corporation (CNOOC) tried to buy Unocal.

Second, the Task Force believes the United States should work with China to encourage a consumption-led growth strategy. China's efforts to construct a "social safety net" are an important element of this. Expenditures on health, welfare, education, and pensions would effectively raise both personal and government consumption and thereby reduce savings. The government should also implement financial reforms to increase access to mortgages, private insurance, car loans, and other forms of consumer finance (including credit cards) to support higher rates of consumption. The United States should share its technical expertise in all of these areas to facilitate China's transition, and the United States should press China to open its financial services sector to greater international competition, introducing best practices and spurring competition in this vital sector of the Chinese economy.

Third, the United States should broaden the discussions regarding China's need to permit its currency to move in response to market forces, as do the currencies of the United States and Europe. Concerned about the impact of currency values on its economic and social stability, China will evaluate any currency adjustment in light of what Japan and other Asian nations may do to change their currency values. The United States should urge the finance ministers of the Asia-Pacific Economic Cooperation Forum or the G20 Finance Ministers to address as a top priority the risks and remedies of the global imbalance. If Asian nations, including China, permitted their currencies to rise with market forces, that would help reduce the imbalances. With respect to China, an appreciation of the yuan would reduce the indirect subsidy given

---

[51] The Trade Adjustment Assistance Act of 2002 does not cover services workers who make up 80 percent of the U.S. workforce or workers who are adversely affected by trade coming from countries with which the United States has no trade agreement. The $10,000 limit on the assistance further curtails the program's usefulness.

Chinese exports and make imported consumer goods less costly, helping to stimulate consumer demand. More important, it would reduce a major cause of bilateral friction with the United States.

Fourth, the Task Force commends the recent efforts by the United States to launch high-level negotiations over trade and economic differences such as exchange-rate flexibility and enforcement of intellectual property rights. These initiatives should be intensified, with the United States presenting clear factual data demonstrating that the policy changes urged are in the mutual interest of both countries. This dialogue should pursue the broad objectives of the recent "Top-to-Bottom Review" of trade relations by the U.S. trade representative.[52] USTR highlights six objectives:

- Integrate China more fully into the global rules-based system of international trade.
- Monitor China's adherence to its WTO obligations more closely.
- Strictly enforce U.S. trade laws.
- Gain further access to the Chinese market and urge greater economic reforms in China.
- Enhance U.S. export promotion efforts.
- Increase efforts to identify and resolve trade issues.

Fifth, to encourage greater respect for intellectual property, the U.S. government should develop a rating system based on one already used by the U.S. Chamber of Commerce to steer U.S. corporations toward provinces that do a better job of protecting IPR. The threat of congressional action can also be a useful catalyst for deliberations with Chinese authorities, but incentives are more likely to succeed than punitive actions, particularly given the competitive nature of the global technology marketplace and the difficulty of negotiating multilateral regimes to punish IPR violators

Sixth, the United States should continue to encourage China to join the WTO Government Procurement Agreement (GPA) and join

---

[52] "U.S.-China Trade Relations: Entering a New Phase of Greater Accountability and Enforcement," U.S. Trade Representative, February 2006.

the World Organization for Animal Health (OIE) as the next steps in China's commitment to international trade arrangements. Having China inside the GPA regime would remove a major obstacle to U.S. exports to China. This is particularly important with respect to an economy like China's, where the government plays an enormous role. Currently, Chinese standards and guidelines on government procurement are skewed in favor of domestic firms.

Seventh, the United States should discourage China from developing regional alternatives to the International Monetary Fund or the WTO that might tend to exclude the United States or discriminate against U.S. firms. In order to do this, the United States should ensure that China's voice is heard in the management of the world's financial mechanisms and that neither the United States nor the international financial institutions themselves neglect the challenges of the Asia-Pacific region.

Finally, the United States and China should develop a road map for integrating China into the G8. Consistent with the notion of China becoming a responsible stakeholder, the United States should promote China's integration with institutions that have an important influence on global affairs. China's track record suggests it is less likely to be out of step with international norms if it is invited to join the norm-setting bodies. Although the G8 is an informal grouping lacking an administrative structure or secretariat, it nonetheless helps coordinate policies among the world's leading economies on a wide range of issues, including public health, law enforcement, foreign affairs, the environment, terrorism, and trade. Chinese participation in the G8, perhaps initially under a "G8 plus one" formula with China as an observer and dialogue partner, would underscore the U.S. desire to see China work in concert with the leading nations of the world on challenges such as global warming and how best to alleviate poverty and promote good governance in Africa. It would strengthen the legitimacy of the G8 by bringing the world's fourth-largest economy into the tent. Moreover, discussions surrounding a Chinese bid for eventual full membership in the G8 would provide a venue at which the United States could encourage China to further its own economic and political reforms.

The Use of Export Controls and Sanctions as Leverage

Export controls and sanctions on the flow of advanced technologies to China offer only limited leverage. The United States should restrict the export of only its most sensitive military and dual-use technologies to China, and it should do so wherever possible in concert with its Asian and European allies. Unilateral sanctions on technology exports are of limited utility, and sanctions on lower-level technology are utterly without purpose, as such technologies are now broadly available. Moreover, the United States should not attempt to use sanctions to shape China's domestic affairs. Sanctions offer insufficient leverage and give the impression that the United States is hostile to China's economic development.

The areas where export restrictions could prove useful as part of an overall U.S. diplomatic strategy include efforts to promote transparency on defense issues and China's cooperation on global nonproliferation. *The United States should offer to relax controls in exchange for Chinese conduct in line with U.S. interests—including greater cooperation on nonproliferation objectives and more transparency on defense issues—and should not hesitate to tighten restrictions if China's foreign policy violates international norms or if it lends support to countries undermining U.S. security interests.*

Enhancing Security Relations

As Robert A. Scalapino has said, the United States should advance its interests in Asia with a strategy that combines both balance-of-power and concert-of-power tactics. *The best way for the United States to ensure that its security interests are not compromised by China's growing military capabilities is to sustain America's space, air, and naval superiority and maintain and enhance its alliances in East Asia.* But even as the United States continues to modernize its own military forces and strengthen security partnerships with China's neighbors, the United States should also promote military dialogue, transparency, and coordination with China.

Sustaining Capabilities

The United States should sustain and selectively enhance its force posture in East Asia, ensuring it has capabilities commensurate with the region's growing importance to the U.S. economy and other vital national interests. Improvements to U.S. military facilities on Guam should continue, not only to relieve some of the burden on Okinawa but also to upgrade the overall capabilities of U.S. Pacific forces. The United States should continue to invest broadly in the next-generation technologies appropriate to the Pacific theater of operations, particularly advanced aerospace and maritime forces. It should also improve the quality of its information collection on and analysis of the Chinese military. This will require training more intelligence specialists with Chinese language skills.

Finally, the United States should also give serious consideration to shifting the balance of its naval forces toward the Pacific from the Atlantic. They are currently divided roughly equally for historical and logistic reasons. The maritime interests of the United States in the future are increasingly in the Asia-Pacific region, and the stationing of its naval forces should be aligned with this trend.

Working with China's Neighbors

Enhancing U.S. security relations with China should not come at the expense of the United States' traditional friends and allies. On the contrary, building mutual understanding and trust with China requires the active support of friends and allies. Because East Asia lacks any effective multilateral security architecture, *the U.S.-led hub-and-spokes alliance system should be strengthened, not discarded.* But it should also be modernized to make room for Chinese participation. The United States should not place its friends and allies in the untenable position of having to "choose" between the United States and China. Specifically, the United States should:

- Continue to make adjustments to the U.S.-Japan alliance, moving gradually away from *exclusive* bilateralism based on common threats toward *extended* bilateralism based on common interests and values;

- Make a conscious effort to find occasions for trilateral discussions among the United States, Japan, and China;

- Work to better coordinate U.S.-South Korea-Japan security planning;

- Give greater attention to ASEAN, the ASEAN Regional Forum, and APEC. In this regard, the United States should appoint a senior official to fill the newly created, congressionally mandated post of U.S. ambassador for ASEAN affairs;

- Work with the members of ASEAN to help draw China into a web of constructive security relationships focused on maritime security and transparency in defense planning and operations and settlement of territorial disputes;

- Sign the Treaty of Amity and Cooperation in Southeast Asia[53] and join the East Asia Summit, if only to ensure continued U.S. influence in all of East Asia's major multilateral structures;

- Strengthen security partnerships in the region, reinvigorating old relationships with Australia, Singapore, Indonesia, and the Philippines, and pursuing new ones with Vietnam and Cambodia;

- Pursue a deeper military partnership with India, but do so consistent with India's own security priorities and in ways that are less likely to come across as militarily threatening to China. Explore the possibilities for U.S.-China-India trilateral security dialogue; and

- Seek to join the SCO as an observer, to help sustain cooperation with Central Asian states in the front lines in the war on terrorism and prevent the SCO from becoming an "anti-U.S." grouping.

The steps listed above will help change the perception that U.S. commitments elsewhere have diminished its interest in Asia, and will also provide opportunities for quiet dialogue with Asian partners on ways to improve U.S.-China relations. The goal is to create a network of formal and informal security relationships in the region that will encourage China to harmonize its foreign policies with those of the United States and the international community.

---

[53] The treaty, first signed in February 1976, specifically and legally binds all its signatories to peaceful coexistence and respect for the principles of sovereignty, territorial integrity, noninterference in internal affairs, and nonuse of force. It is one of the basic documents of ASEAN, and only states that have signed the treaty are eligible to join the East Asia Summit. The sixteen states that attended the first East Asia Summit in December 2005 included the ten members of ASEAN plus China, Japan, South Korea, India, Australia, and New Zealand.

Building Mutual Understanding and Cooperation

A primary objective of enhancing U.S.-China security relations is to reach an understanding with China that the U.S. military position in Asia and U.S. alliances do not seek to threaten China or seek to constrain China's ability to develop peacefully. Given the huge military advantage currently enjoyed by the United States, and given China's strong prioritization of domestic growth and stability over foreign adventures, the Task Force believes that the United States can develop strong security ties to China that reduce the likelihood of unhealthy competition and will serve both nations' interests.

With respect to China's aspirations for great power status, the United States will have to find ways to signal that it is prepared to welcome a growing role for China in regional and global security affairs even as it seeks Beijing's understanding and appreciation for a continued U.S. leadership role. One way to do this is to invite China to observe and participate in U.S.-led alliance activities. This should be done on a reciprocal basis, leveraging invitations to participate in exercises such as Cobra Gold in Thailand for U.S. access to Russia-China bilateral exercises or SCO regional security activities.

A secondary objective of enhancing security ties is to expand cooperation with China on the many areas of common military concern, including regional stability broadly construed, combating terrorism and piracy, responding to regional humanitarian disasters, and supporting UN peacekeeping operations.

Forging a closer security relationship with China requires building habits of cooperation and coordination as a mechanism for reducing mutual suspicions and broadening mutual interests. The United States should initiate a sustained high-level military strategic dialogue to complement the Senior Dialogue launched at the deputy secretary-vice foreign minister level in 2005 and the Strategic Economic Dialogue launched by Treasury Secretary Henry M. Paulson Jr. in 2006.

In its security dialogue with China, the United States should:

- Energize the nuclear dialogue announced by President Bush and President Hu in April 2006 to better understand each other's nuclear doctrines, including the roles and capabilities of offensive and defensive systems and ways to avoid an arms race in space.

- Continue to encourage transparency in defense planning, procurement, and budgeting.

- Press for "value-based" reciprocity from the PLA in exchanges, including that the PLA allow visits to diverse locations in China and make available top-quality PRC personnel from a range of professional tracks.

- Build on the practices developed in less controversial exchanges to expand cooperation into areas with a higher military content, such as consultation on events on the Korean Peninsula (e.g., the explosion near the Yalu River two years ago or maritime incidents) and counterproliferation.

- Include on the agenda crisis management discussions of how to handle incidents involving the military forces of the two countries, learning lessons from the EP-3 incident.

As it builds a more substantive military dialogue with China, the United States should also pursue greater functional cooperation with China in the realm of international security to include the following types of missions:

- international search and rescue;
- multilateral humanitarian relief;
- counterterrorism operations;
- nonproliferation operations;
- noncombatant evacuation;
- counterpiracy, narcotics, and human smuggling operations; and
- UN and other multilateral peacekeeping operations.

Military Dialogue

The recommendation for expanded security dialogue merits some elaboration. The United States should strive to reach an understanding that each party's force modernization program will be tailored to avoid moves that might threaten the other party's core security interests. As envisioned by the Task Force, the security dialogue would stop short of formal arms control talks—something the Task Force considers unrealistic for many reasons, including the power disparities between the United States and China, alliance obligations, and the difficulty of limiting U.S. forces capable of striking China without jeopardizing Washington's ability to fulfill its global commitments. Nonetheless, the talks should have a strategic quality, with a strong focus on strategic systems—nuclear arms and missile defenses. The dialogue should include discussion of what restraints the two sides are prepared to offer each other in the development of their strategic posture. Expert-level talks would focus on a host of issues, including the following:

- the international nuclear environment;
- nuclear doctrines;
- missile defenses and China's missile buildup opposite Taiwan;
- escalation control in the event of a crisis;
- nuclear force levels and composition; and
- advanced conventional power projections systems such as air refueling fleets, naval amphibious task groups, airborne operations, and global surveillance and reconnaissance systems.

Allaying mutual suspicions and encouraging China to modulate its conventional and nuclear defense modernization to stay in tune with Beijing's self-proclaimed limited national security objectives and thereby reduce the pressure on the United States to increase its own force posture will not be easy. For example, should the United States provide assurances to China that U.S. missile defense capabilities will not neutralize China's deterrent and provide data to prove it? With what conditions? The Task Force recommends that the United States use the newly launched dialogue on strategic nuclear issues to delve into this issue, and that the United States should stand ready to share data on missile defenses with China provided that China reciprocates by sharing information on the goals and scope of its own strategic forces modernization.

Preserving Peace and Stability across the Taiwan Strait

Since Nixon's trip to China, Taiwan has dominated security relations between Washington and Beijing. The Task Force recommends that the United States enhance current efforts under way designed to reduce tension across the strait and minimize the corrosive influence of the Taiwan question on U.S.-China relations. Attempts to formulate a new "Communiqué" with China or to devise a formal "interim agreement" on the status of Taiwan are likely to cause more problems than they would solve. *The policies of "dual restraint" and "dual assurance" should continue, deterring Chinese aggression and opposing Taiwan's steps toward independence while at the same time assuring China that the United States does not seek to perpetuate Taiwan's separation from the mainland and assuring Taiwan that the United States does not seek to pressure it into negotiating a final resolution.* The ingredients of this approach include:

- Maintaining strong, forward-deployed armed forces in East Asia and making it clear to Beijing that the United States is prepared to live up to its security-related obligations under the Taiwan Relations Act.[54]

- Opposing unilateral changes to the status quo by the PRC or Taiwan.

- Continuing to sell arms (including missile defense systems) to Taiwan designed to enhance its ability to deter a Chinese attack and resist Chinese coercion.

- Continuing to communicate to Taiwan that it should make necessary improvements in its defense capabilities to deter Chinese aggression and that it should spend its defense resources wisely while opposing any effort by Taiwan to acquire an offensive deterrent, especially nuclear weapons.

- Insisting that any resolution of cross-strait issues be peaceful and noncoercive.

The Task Force recommends that the United States make its stance on Taiwan more explicit. China should understand clearly that the

---

[54] SEC. 3 (a) of the Taiwan Relations Act states: In furtherance of the policy set forth in section 2 of this Act, the United States will make available to Taiwan such defense articles and defense services in such quantity as may be necessary to enable Taiwan to maintain a sufficient self-defense capability. SEC. 3 (c) states: (c) The president is directed to inform Congress promptly of any threat to the security or the social or economic system of the people on Taiwan and any danger to the interests of the United States arising there from. The president and Congress shall determine, in accordance with constitutional processes, appropriate action by the United States in response to any such danger.

United States does not rule out using force to thwart any Chinese attempt to compel unification through force. Similarly, the United States should make clear to Taiwan's government that Washington does not support Taiwan independence and that Taiwan cannot count on U.S. military intervention if it provokes a crisis.

Moreover, given the potential volatility of the cross-strait situation, there are some modest steps the United States could take to encourage closer cross-strait relations. The United States should:

- Continue to urge China and Taiwan to lower the rhetorical temperature; build practical links in trade, travel, and communication; and hold direct political dialogue on an equal footing, without preconditions.

- Encourage cross-strait military confidence and security building measures.

- Continue to host Track II trilateral meetings to allow academics, retired civil and military officials, and public figures from Taiwan, the PRC, and the United States to discuss relations in a low-key setting, forging relationships and hopefully reducing the likelihood of miscommunication and miscalculation. At least three such initiatives have been under way for several years.

- Decline to act as a mediator between Taipei and Beijing or to endorse specific formulas for resolving cross-strait differences. Indeed, such steps could be counterproductive. At the same time, remain open to acting as a facilitator if both sides request it.

Finally, the Task Force notes that the Stanley Foundation has launched a Track II dialogue involving participants from the United States, China, and Japan to discuss possible confidence- and security-building measures. The United States should adopt any ideas generated by this initiative that it deems might help reduce the risk of miscommunication or miscalculation in a Taiwan crisis.

China-Japan

The U.S.-Japan alliance remains the cornerstone of the United States' Pacific system of alliances, and the United States depends on the alliance to help advance U.S. interests not only in East Asia, but also beyond. The United States should continue to strengthen the U.S.-Japan alliance to cope with the full range of challenges of the post-Cold War world.

In order for a strategy of integrating China into the community of nations to succeed, the United States must work in concert with its Japanese ally. So long as Sino-Japanese relations are marred by deep mistrust, Japan's ability to assist in China's integration will remain limited and efforts by Japan to play a more active role in global security affairs—efforts championed by the United States—will tend to cause alarm in Beijing. It is therefore in the interest of the United States for Japan and China to build more cooperative relations. The core differences between Tokyo and Beijing involve questions of honor, history, national self-esteem, and fear, as well as a competition for power and influence. These are all issues that the two parties themselves will ultimately need to resolve bilaterally—or at least come to some accommodation. But the United States has a role to play. The United States should:

- Encourage dialogue between Tokyo and Beijing aimed at resolving differences and achieving genuine reconciliation in a spirit of mutual respect.

- Urge both countries to identify areas of common interest—trade and investment, nuclear energy, the environment, counterterrorism—and build on those, rather than focus on differences.

- Embrace Japan's ambition to become a more effective, engaged, global citizen, and quietly express Washington's view that in order for Japan to assume this broader international role it will be necessary for Tokyo to improve its relations with Beijing and Seoul.

- While staying out of territorial disputes, offer "good offices" to facilitate Sino-Japanese dialogue on areas of mutual interest, such as maritime security, energy security, counterterrorism, and nonproliferation.

Strengthening Nonproliferation Efforts

The United States currently confronts two distinct nonproliferation challenges: North Korea and Iran. It is critical to secure Chinese cooperation on both. Looking ahead more broadly, the United States needs

China to reinforce nonproliferation norms with others as well as obeying them itself.

The United States should continue to work with China on the North Korea problem even if the two nations sometimes prioritize their interests differently or employ different tactics. Finding a solution demands a combination of more "Asian sticks" and "American carrots." The recent progress is encouraging, but everyone acknowledges that it represents the first steps, "the beginning of the beginning." To help encourage China to play the constructive role that has been especially evident over the past year, the United States should add a strategic element to its North Korea policy:

- In close coordination with South Korea and Japan, the United States should seek to develop a consensus with China on long-term goals for the peninsula, namely, that permanent peace be established on the Korean Peninsula and that the North and South then be given support to unify on their own terms and in their own time, without nuclear weapons, and without large American forward-stationed ground forces.

Some of the same techniques the United States could usefully employ to forge closer cooperation with China on the North Korea challenge should also be applied in the case of Iran. China's interests with Iran and those of the United States are not aligned, even though there are points of congruence. China opposes Iran's development of nuclear weapons, but feels no particular threat from Iran's nuclear activities. China may not even be convinced that Iran is seeking to develop nuclear weapons. China is also seeking to increase its own influence in the Middle East, especially with Iran, a nation rich in oil with which China also has deep historical ties and significant contemporary economic, political, and military points of connection. China does not share the U.S. government's antipathy for the Iranian government, and China has made clear its opposition to the imposition of sanctions on Iran. As has been the case with North Korea, the United States will need to do many things in order to convince China to cooperate more closely with U.S. and EU efforts to rein in Iran's nuclear ambitions, including presenting convincing evidence of Iran's nuclear weapons ambitions; demonstrating a willingness to seek a diplomatic solution to the problem (including direct talks with Iranian officials); placing its top priority on the nuclear issue (as opposed to other aspects of Iran's conduct that the United States finds troubling); and showing a sensitivity to legitimate Chinese interests (such as China's heavy reliance on Iranian oil exports to meet its energy needs).

Ultimately, the cases of North Korea and Iran highlight the need to foster closer cooperation with China on a global nonproliferation agenda. The targeted application of sanctions against Chinese firms that violate U.S. nonproliferation laws can help deter irresponsible conduct by specific companies, but does little to foster broader Chinese government support for U.S. nonproliferation objectives. The United States and China should discuss ways to strengthen the Nuclear Nonproliferation Treaty, including how to enhance global controls on the production and stockpiling of fissile material. The United States should expand contact with China's arms control bureaucracy, sharing appropriately safeguarded intelligence information to facilitate cooperative nonproliferation initiatives, particularly efforts to keep nuclear weapons out of the hands of terrorists. The United States should also provide more training opportunities for China's arms control specialists.

Encouraging Political Reform, Rule of Law, and Respect for Human Rights

A strategy of integration must include efforts to encourage China's progress toward greater respect for international norms of human rights, including political liberty and religious freedom. Encouraging greater respect for the rule of law, human rights, and progress toward democratization in China will take time: all the more reason for the United States to work diligently and consistently on these objectives. There are many forces at work driving China toward greater pluralism, but China's leaders are resisting fundamental political reforms, considering them a threat to the legitimacy of the CCP as well as to China's future economic growth and social stability. The United States should make the opposite argument: Greater respect for human rights will help ensure China's economic growth, social stability, and political legitimacy, not undermine it. The U.S. approach to human rights needs to be multifaceted.

First, the United States should today rededicate itself to leading by example. The United States' ability to champion a human rights agenda with China has been severely impaired by the U.S. failure to live up to its own ideals of the rule of law and respect for human rights. The audience for U.S. advocacy for human rights is not simply the Chinese government, but the Chinese people themselves. The Chinese people will ultimately be the architects of political reform and the most effective advocates of human rights in China. The American government is not the only, and often not the most effective, means for advancing liberal ideas and ideals. Nongovernmental organizations, universities, corporations, individual citizens, international organizations, the Internet, and many other means can be effective in conveying expected norms of behavior to China. Compared to authoritarian regimes of the past, China is much more open to outside influences.

Second, as a practical matter, the United States can best advance human rights inside China by helping China to build institutions that are instrumental to making government more transparent and accountable to the people, including a strong civil society; a free, responsible media; and a professional, independent judiciary. The United States should expand training and outreach programs in all of these areas, not only at the national level, but also at the local level where practices often lag behind those embraced, at least on paper, by national-level authorities. U.S. government funding for such efforts should be continued and expanded. The United States should do so even while recognizing that its goals and those of the Chinese may well differ even as both sides collaborate, with China hoping reforms will consolidate the power and effectiveness of the CCP and the United States hoping reforms will help to open up the legal and political systems and make them more accountable to the Chinese people.

Third, as the largest consumer of the products of Chinese labor, the U.S. government and the American people have a legitimate interest in the conditions of Chinese labor. American corporations should continue to develop corporate social responsibility (CSR) programs that can assure U.S. consumers that the products they buy are produced in compliance with international and Chinese law. As the U.S. government did with "dolphin-safe" tuna labels, the government should explore ways to promote those products and services produced in China by firms adhering to the highest international standards of labor rights and environmental protection, allowing market forces to help drive improvements in labor conditions.

Fourth, when the United States chooses to criticize China's conduct, it should do so not only in frank private talks as part of the bilateral agenda, but also in the appropriate public multilateral venues—such as at the UN Human Rights Council in Geneva—with a strong focus on norms and protocols. This is more than a presentational issue. China has committed itself to a range of international standards and obligations regarding the treatment of its citizens. The U.S. case to support human rights is made stronger by its ability to remind China of its international obligations, and to make clear that the United States will hold China to the same standards of behavior as it does other nations.

Fifth, the United States should discourage Chinese attempts to censor or control the Internet. U.S. support for Voice of America, Radio Free Asia, and other efforts to broadcast news and information to the Chinese audience should be intensified if China fails to relax media controls. In cooperation with private-sector Internet service providers, the United States should lead a multilateral effort to establish a code of conduct for operating the Internet, to include an examination of controls on content and protection of privacy rights.

In general, when approaching China on human rights issues, the U.S. approach should cast support for a more open, transparent, and humane society in terms of helping China realize its own goals of promoting economic growth, enhancing social stability, creating a harmonious society, improving relations with Taiwan, and bolstering its standing in the international community. The United States should also frankly point out that so long as U.S. and Chinese perspectives on human rights issues diverge, there will be an upper ceiling on the partnership the United States seeks to build with China as a responsible stakeholder in the international community.

Tibet

On Tibet, the Task Force recommends that the United States continue to encourage Beijing to talk directly to the Dalai Lama and welcome him back to China, noting that he is a proponent of nonviolence and has given up the pursuit of independence for Tibet at considerable political risk. This call for dialogue should be elevated and put on the agenda for a summit meeting. Moreover, the U.S. Tibet policy coordinator should renew efforts to make an official visit to Tibet to examine conditions there. China seems to pursue its dialogue with representatives of the Dalai Lama only when its failure to do so would risk internationalizing the issue and tarnishing its global reputation.

Education

One of the more important, but less obvious, steps the United States can take to enhance its ability to influence China is to educate Americans in Chinese studies and to expand America's educational exchange programs with China. Accordingly, the United States should launch a major new initiative to strengthen the nation's ability to understand and interact with China on the fiftieth anniversary of the 1958 National Defense Education Act (NDEA). This new NDEA would:

- Fund a comprehensive national educational plan designed to train a new generation of Americans about China's language, history, economy, politics, and culture. Numerous educational institutions are continuing and expanding these programs, not only at the collegiate level, but also in primary and secondary education, often with cooperation from nongovernmental organizations (like the Asia Society) and corporations. The Task Force recommends that federal funding for these efforts should be significantly increased.

- Dramatically increase the number of scholarships available to qualified Chinese students seeking postgraduate education in the United States. History teaches that these students will be in the vanguard of political and economic reform in the decades ahead.

Protecting the Global Environment and Promoting Sustainable Energy Policies

Energy and the environment are two of the more promising areas for China and the United States to build on their common interests. The fate of the planet depends on the success of efforts by the United States and China to curb harmful emissions and work together, as the world's largest developed country and the world's largest developing country, to demonstrate that environmental protection and economic growth are not mutually incompatible. The United States should call on China to demonstrate that it is a responsible member of the international community by joining global efforts to combat climate change.

The United States will find that China is more receptive to cooperation on climate change if it perceives that the United States itself is dedicated to environmental protection—cooperating with international efforts to reduce greenhouse emissions, providing incentives to business and consumers for the introduction of "green" technologies in manufacturing and building design, promoting conservation and recycling, improving automobile fuel efficiency, promoting hybrid and other eco-friendly low-emissions vehicles, and funding basic research on alternative energy sources. *The United States cannot expect China to participate in global efforts to combat climate change if the U.S. government does not itself fully and unequivocally accept the link between human activity and global warming and join with other nations to seek multilateral solutions.*

As the world's two largest energy consumers and two largest producers of greenhouse gases, the United States and China share an interest in affordable, ecologically sustainable energy. The fact that the United States is a world leader in many of the relevant technologies makes collaboration in this area doubly attractive, as it could help reduce the U.S. trade deficit with China while simultaneously keeping energy costs in check and cleaning up the environment. During Treasury Secretary Paulson's December 2006 visit to Beijing, for instance, China announced it had chosen Toshiba and its U.S.-based Westinghouse subsidiary to construct the first four of what may prove to be dozens of new nuclear power reactors, a deal estimated to be worth $6 billion to $10 billion, not counting possible follow-on sales and servicing agreements. But this is just the tip of the iceberg. [55]

---

[55] The opportunities are truly boundless. To give just one example: Berkeley Lab scientists led by Shih-Ger (Ted) Chang have developed a potentially cheap and efficient way of removing mercury from coal-fired power plant emissions. The technique could help prevent the toxic element from entering the environment and a food chain that culminates at the dinner table. Although Chang's mercury-slashing technique is still under development—it was recently

Accordingly, the Task Force recommends that the United States significantly enhance cooperation between the Department of Energy and China's National Development and Reform Commission and between the National Academy of Sciences and its Chinese counterpart. Fruitful areas for cooperative research and development and the introduction of new technologies to China include:

- "clean" coal power plants and advanced boiling-water nuclear reactors;

- energy-efficient light bulbs and appliances;

- solar power technology and related applications;

- hybrid and hydrogen automobile drive systems; and

- advanced systems to reduce harmful emissions from industrial facilities.

The Task Force also recommends that the United States encourage China's inclusion in multilateral energy dialogues among oil-consuming nations, including facilitating China's integration and eventual membership in the International Energy Agency (IEA). China is not a member of the Organization for Economic Cooperation and Development (OECD), the parent organization of the IEA, and China does not currently have a ninety-day strategic petroleum reserve—another requirement of IEA membership (China has about forty-five days' supply). Nonetheless, through "implementing agreements," China could cooperate with the IEA in a number of fields, including energy technologies, environmental protection, energy efficiency, and diversification. The United States, in concert with China and Japan, should also explore ways of creating an East Asia regional energy stockpile from which member nations could draw supply in an emergency.[56]

---

licensed to an East Bay engineering firm called Mobotec USA, where it will undergo pilot-scale testing—early lab-based experiments indicate that it possesses the hallmarks of a successful pollution control technology.

[56] For a useful analysis of the energy issue in U.S.-China relations and of the issue of China's possible membership in the IEA, see Kenneth Lieberthal and Mikkal Herberg, "China's Search for Energy Security: Implications for U.S. Policy," The National Bureau of Asian Research Analysis, Volume 17, No. 1, April 2006.

Conclusion

The preceding analysis attempts to take stock of where China is and where it is headed, focusing on the implications of China's course on the interests of the United States. China's progress over the past three decades has been staggering. The Chinese people today enjoy an overall standard of living far superior to that of previous generations, and China's rapid economic growth is likely to continue. China will play proud host to the 2008 Olympics, eager to show off what they have accomplished through reform and opening up.

And yet the problems facing China are immense. It will take considerable time, attention, and resources for China to address them effectively. Consequently, China's leaders require and desire peace and stability at home and abroad (particularly on China's periphery) to provide the strategic breathing room to address the nation's domestic challenges.

Accordingly, China's leaders need to maintain stable, if not amicable, relations with the United States, the world's preeminent power. China will try to take steps the United States wants it to take in order to maintain friendly bilateral relations unless those steps collide with China's view of what it must do to maintain domestic stability, national security, and economic growth. The United States cannot shy away from the areas where its interests and those of China diverge. The United States must stand ready, even to use military force if necessary, to safeguard its vital security interests. But most of its interests will be best protected if the United States can develop and implement strategies that maximize the areas of common interest with China and minimize areas where interests diverge.

Since President Nixon opened the door to China, the United States has benefited greatly from that relationship, both economically and strategically. China has as well. But in the post-11/9 and post-9/11 era of globalization (after the fall of the Berlin Wall on November 9, 1989, and the terrorist attacks of September 11, 2001), while the points of convergence have increased, a political consensus about the appropriate policy toward China has come under strain. Rebuilding that consensus should be a major priority of the U.S. government, and specifically of the president, because the challenges confronting the United States today—whether combating terrorism, limiting the proliferation and spread of weapons of mass destruction, reining in North Korea's nuclear ambitions, ensuring energy security, or protecting the global environment—will be more effectively managed with China's cooperation than without. Indeed, many cannot be managed without China's active and constructive participation. The challenges of today are equally compelling as those confronted during the Cold War, and the United States learned then that advancing its interests requires friends and partners.

China's future is uncertain. The United States can discern the landscape—China requires peace and stability internationally and cooperation with the United States to continue to grow and deal with its pressing domestic problems. But even the Chinese people themselves cannot know for sure which paths China will walk down. For the United States, the objective is clear: Further integrating China into the global community offers the best hope of shaping China's interests and conduct in accordance with international norms on security, trade and finance, and human rights, and encouraging collaboration to confront the challenges both countries face. The United States needs to invest heavily to maximize the areas of cooperation with China and minimize the likelihood of conflict. The ultimate security of the United States lies in the deep foundations of U.S. national power—military, political, economic, and moral—which the Task Force believes can be sustained, giving the United States ample time and means to evaluate and adjust policies toward China in the event that proves necessary. The United States should approach China with an affirmative agenda from a position of confidence.

Additional and Dissenting Views

I agree with the analysis, the findings, and the recommendations of the report. At the same time, my sense is that its tone is somewhat too sanguine; China and the United States will find it difficult to manage the relationship during the next few decades in a way that avoids an adversarial outcome. The overriding goals of China's leadership appear to be: First, to maintain its party's domestic monopoly of political power; second (and related), to preserve China's internal stability and peaceful economic growth; third, to translate that growth over time into a position of global power, redressing what it rightly sees as a 150-year chronicle of weakness and of oppression by outsiders.

The history of relations between the established power and the rising one is not encouraging. In the case that is the focus of this report, there are already important elements in each country that regard the other as dedicated to repressing its rise, in one case, or undermining or supplanting it, in the other. The close and intensifying economic ties are as likely to be the occasion of dispute as a reason to cooperate politically. Though there are common interests (e.g., opposing WMD proliferation), there are also conflicting ones (e.g., relative influence in Northeast Asia). And the vast difference in political systems both exacerbates the other frictions and makes it more difficult to deal with particular disputes.

None of this makes an adversarial outcome inevitable. But it does suggest a need to display considerably more understanding of the issues and skill in handling them than has been the case for recent administrations if the admittedly limited effect that the United States can have on the evolution and development of Chinese policy is to be a positive one. Chinese internal developments, whose future path is, as the final paragraph of the report states, unknown even to the Chinese people, will be the most important factor in determining whether the rise will indeed be peaceful.

Harold Brown
joined by
Arthur Waldron

While I concur with many of the Task Force report's observations about China's remarkable achievements and current challenges, I disagree on two central strategic issues.

The report notes, correctly, that U.S. policy must combine elements of engagement (or integration) with efforts to balance China's growing power, but it understates the difficulty of the latter task. Thanks to a sustained, broad buildup, China has already increased its ability to challenge American military preponderance in the Western Pacific. Maintaining a favorable balance of power will not be easy, especially at a time when U.S. attention and resources are likely to remain divided between Asia and the Middle East.

Nor is this merely a matter of military competition. China's economic expansion is enhancing its ability to woo its neighbors (including some traditional American friends) and to promote new regional institutions that aim to marginalize the United States. Even as they talk and trade, the United States and China are thus engaged in a serious strategic rivalry. It would be a mistake to exaggerate this aspect of what remains a complex and mixed relationship, but neither can it be ignored or wished away.

In my view the Task Force report also downplays the importance of the deep political differences that separate Washington and Beijing. These impose real limits on the ability of the two sides to build a "close, candid, and cooperative relationship." The American people are never going to fully trust a government that restricts freedom of religion, speech, and political competition. For their part, China's current rulers will continue to fear that the United States aims to displace them by encouraging "peaceful evolution" toward democracy. Until there is a greater commonality of values between the two Pacific powers, any convergence of interests will remain limited and tenuous. Excessive optimism about what can be accomplished risks raising false hopes and setting the stage for disappointment and eventual backlash.

Aaron L. Friedberg

I have signed the report because as a total document, there are many sections that address issues between the United States and China that can lead to a better understanding, and hence a better relationship. A frank discussion of our objectives and those of China can only be helpful.

Where I disagree with this report, however, is the persistent urging of democracy in China. I have been going to China since 1975 and have seen unbelievable change not just in the economy but in the lives of the people.

Every country has its own culture and comes by its political system through its own history. In my opinion, democracy cannot be obtained by outside pressure on a nation but only adopted from within. In the case of China, I doubt that the incredible progress they have made since the end of the Cultural Revolution could have occurred if there were political turmoil in China.

We should stop pressing China to adopt a democratic political system—that is up to the Chinese. If it is to occur, it has to be their own choice.

A dialogue at senior levels is essential to better understand each other's intentions on important issues. Transparency is essential. Both nations must understand that there are likely always to be differences on a number of issues. That should not, however, deter a constructive relationship between the United States and China.

Maurice R. Greenberg
joined by
Herbert Levin

Although I generally endorse the analysis and recommendations contained in this report, I wish that some additional issues in the relationship had been considered in greater detail.

One of the issues neglected is the rise of economic nationalism in China. This is reflected in tighter restrictions on foreign ownership in strategic sectors of the economy, increasing complaints that foreign firms have acquired too large a market share or control too many patents, and what appears to be the selective targeting of foreign firms for violations of Chinese laws and regulations. Economic nationalism is also reflected in Chinese government efforts to promote "national champions" in key industries, such as the recent announcement that the Chinese aerospace industry would be encouraged to compete with Boeing and Airbus in the manufacture of passenger aircraft.

Together, these trends raise the concern that the business climate inside China is becoming less favorable for some foreign firms, and that the United States and multinational corporations will encounter increasing Chinese competition in their home markets and in third-country markets as well. In part, these consequences stem from the normal interfirm competition that develops when a large economy like China's modernizes successfully. But, more worryingly, they also reflect a deliberate policy of the Chinese government to limit opportunities for foreign firms in China and to promote the interests of Chinese firms operating abroad.

Another issue that might have received greater emphasis is the increase in transnational organized crime that operates in or from China. This involves drug trafficking, smuggling of various products to or from China (such as timber to China and pirated CDs and counterfeit fashions from China), illegal emigration, and trafficking in persons (particularly women). This is an emerging issue that should form the basis of extensive cooperation among China, the United States, and other foreign governments.

A final issue that I wish had been given greater attention is the need for improvement in the ways in which Americans understand China and discuss our policy toward China. The report proposes a program to promote education about China in schools and universities, and I support that recommendation—although I would broaden it to include international affairs more generally. Equally important, however, is the need to improve the way in which China is discussed in public forums and in the U.S. policy community. Too often, policy discourse portrays China in black-or-white terms that fail to reflect that country's complexity and diversity. Too often, public discussion presents exaggerated and unconditional forecasts for China—that it will collapse, that it will democratize, that it will seek hegemony in Asia—that do not adequately acknowledge the real uncertainties about China's future. Too often, the debate over China becomes polarized and ad hominem, with participants disparaged as "apologists" or "cold warriors." If we are to address the challenges and opportunities posed by China effectively, then our understanding of that country needs to be as informed and sophisticated as possible, and the debate as sharp and rational as it can be.

Harry Harding
joined by
Arthur Waldron

Looking toward the future of U.S.-China relations, this report carefully considers reasons both for optimism and concern. We in the United States must remember that each forward step taken by the Chinese government can only come with parallel reform of U.S. policy. The future of a mutually beneficial relationship will be secured by dialogue, not colonial lecturing and double standards.

As a fundamental requirement for promoting cross-cultural understanding and dialogue between China and the United States, this report recommends increased investment in programs that promote Chinese studies. Organizations like the China Institute have long focused on this issue, starting language programs for children at age three and expanding high school exchange programs in Beijing to educate a new generation in Chinese studies. Spreading Chinese language ability and building cross-cultural awareness will be the key to ensuring future peace and prosperity in a world where China and the United States work together as equal partners.

Virginia Ann Kamsky

U.S. presidents have peacefully managed the modern relationship with China since it was initiated by Nixon. Clinton rerouted U.S. Navy ships as a deterrent to violence when the PRC tested warhead-less missiles in the Taiwan Strait. He defeated protectionists and human rights extremists in the United States when they sought to hold hostage China's WTO membership to their unrealistic goals.

Similarly, President Bush has reiterated the United States' "One China Policy," and approved arms sales to Taiwan while making it clear that the United States would not be dragged into a confrontation with China by independence provocations from Taipei.

Future presidents of both parties will need support as they resist military containment zealots, economic protectionists, and those Americans who perceive modern China as so odious it must be confronted by the United States at every turn. This will require diplomacy-supporting, statesmanlike presidential leadership. The unique period since World War II when the United States dominated East Asia is slowly ending, and historically precedented relationships are reemerging; these will not be inimical to U.S. interests if we comprehend the process and skillfully participate in it.

Herbert Levin

I endorse this report because on the whole it captures the complexity and contradictions of the Chinese landscape and Sino-American relation; and proposes a positive but realistic agenda and policy course. I agree with the bulk of the analysis, conclusions, and recommendations. But I have some significant differences and reservations, including the following:

- The leading summary assessment of China's international behavior (page 7) is too benign—i.e., "growing adherence to international rules," and becoming "more attentive to U.S. views." The picture is more mixed—indeed the report itself details many areas where Chinese policies are inimical or at least equivocal with respect to international standards and American interests.

- The report seriously understates the harshness of the Chinese political system and the backsliding in recent years on political reform and human rights.
- Although the study has much good material on our trade problems with China, the cumulative impression left by this section is one of insufficient urgency about a daily deficit of some $700 million.
- I believe that the nature of China's political system will importantly shape its international behavior in future decades. The more open, humane, and democratic China becomes, the more likely it will be cooperative rather than disruptive on the world stage. The report does not make this connection, and thereby underplays the importance of encouraging political reform and human rights.

Winston Lord
joined by
Randy Schriver and
Arthur Waldron

This report has strengths I endorse, but I also disagree on some key questions. To summarize:

First, the report does not face squarely the fundamental illegitimacy and grave weaknesses of the Chinese regime nor the likelihood that it will change, sooner or later, perhaps without warning, and quite possibly catching Washington by surprise.

Second, the report gives insufficient weight to China's current military buildup, which has already sparked an arms race in Asia, the logic of which may lead to the acquisition of nuclear weapons by Japan and other states.

Third, I find the economic analysis misleading and overly positive.

Fourth, I believe that Taiwan will continue to exist as an independent state and that therefore Washington (which has never recognized Chinese sovereignty over Taiwan), China, and the rest of the world should start thinking about how we will accommodate it.

Finally, I remember the USSR. Sixteen years ago Moscow freed speech and the media, legalized political opposition parties, instituted elections for parliament and presidency, and assured property rights. The ruble has since been made fully convertible.

If China is genuinely to succeed, it will have to follow suit. If Beijing reforms at the roots, as Moscow did, then prospects for relations with the United States are bright. If, however, the Party attempts (as now) to hold on to absolute power at all costs, the danger of instability and conflict in China and the region will become serious.

I address these views in further detail elsewhere: www.history.upenn.edu/docs/waldron_task_force.pdf.

Arthur Waldron

Task Force Members

Roger C. Altman served two tours of duty in the U.S. Treasury Department, initially serving President Carter as assistant secretary for domestic finance and later serving President Clinton as deputy secretary. Since 1996, Mr. Altman has served as chairman and co-chief executive officer of Evercore Partners, which has become the most active investment banking boutique in the world. Previously, he was vice chairman of the Blackstone Group and responsible for its investment banking business. His initial Wall Street career involved Lehman Brothers, where he eventually became cohead of investment banking, as well as a member of the firm's management committee and of its board of directors. Mr. Altman is a trustee of New York-Presbyterian Hospital, New Visions for Public Schools, and the American Museum of Natural History, where he also serves as chairman of the investment committee. He also is a member of the Council on Foreign Relations and serves on its finance and investment committee. He received an AB from Georgetown University and an MBA from the University of Chicago.

Peter E. Bass is managing director and chief of staff at Promontory Financial Group, LLC, a consulting firm for global financial services companies. He was previously a vice president at Goldman Sachs, responsible for international government affairs and chief of staff to the firm's president and co-chief operating officer. Prior to his private sector

---

Note: Task Force members participate in their individual and not their institutional capacities.
*The individual has endorsed the report and submitted an additional or a dissenting view.

career, Mr. Bass was a career civil servant for over ten years, holding a number of senior positions at the Department of State and the National Security Council, including deputy assistant secretary of state for energy, sanctions and commodities; and executive assistant to the national security adviser.

Dennis C. Blair will hold the Omar Bradley Chair of Strategic Leadership at the Army War College and Dickinson College for 2007–2008. From 2003 to 2006 he was president and CEO of the Institute for Defense Analyses (IDA), a federally funded research and development center based in Alexandria, Virginia. Prior to retiring from the Navy in 2002, he served as commander in chief, U.S. Pacific Command, the largest of the combatant commands. During his thirty-four-year Navy career, Admiral Blair served on guided missile destroyers in both the Atlantic and Pacific fleets and commanded the Kitty Hawk Battle Group. Ashore, he served as director of the joint staff and as the first associate director of Central Intelligence for Military Support. He has also served in budget and policy positions on the National Security Council and several major Navy staffs.

Harold Brown* is currently a counselor and trustee at the Center for Strategic and International Studies (CSIS); a partner at Warburg Pincus LLC; and on the board of Evergreen Holdings, Inc. and the Altria Group Inc. Previously, he was chairman of the Foreign Policy Institute of the Johns Hopkins University Paul H. Nitze School of Advanced International Studies. He was president of the California Institute of Technology from 1969 to 1977 and has served in a number of senior government positions including secretary of defense from 1977 to 1981.

Ashton B. Carter is codirector (with former Secretary of Defense William J. Perry) of the Preventive Defense Project and chair of the International Relations, Security, and Science faculty at Harvard's John F. Kennedy School of Government. Dr. Carter served as assistant secretary of defense for international security policy during President Clinton's first term. Dr. Carter was twice awarded the Department of Defense Distinguished Service Medal, the highest award given by the department. For his contributions to intelligence, he was awarded the Defense Intelligence Medal.

Charles W. Freeman III is managing director of the China Alliance of Independent Law Firms. He was until late 2005 the assistant U.S. trade representative for China affairs, responsible for developing and implementing overall U.S. trade policy toward China, Taiwan, Hong Kong, Macao, and Mongolia. He earlier served as international affairs counsel to U.S. Senator Frank Murkowski (R–AK), concentrating on trade and international finance and energy issues. He joined government service after ten years in the private and nonprofit sectors as a lawyer and emerging market venture capitalist in Boston; Asia–Pacific conference director with the *International Herald Tribune*; and economic program director with the Asia Foundation in Hong Kong. He is a member of the board of directors of the National Committee on U.S.-China Relations.

Aaron L. Friedberg* is professor of politics and international affairs at Princeton University, where he has taught since 1987. In 2003–2005 he served in the Office of the Vice President as a deputy assistant for national security affairs. He is a member of the secretary of state's advisory committee on democracy promotion. From 2001–2002 he was the first Henry A. Kissinger scholar at the Library of Congress.

Paul Gewirtz is the Potter Stewart professor of constitutional law at Yale Law School and the director of the China Law Center. He teaches and writes in a wide range of legal fields. The China Law Center carries out research and teaching, and also undertakes a large number of cooperative projects with government and academic institutions in China on key legal and policy reform issues. While on leave from Yale at the U.S. Department of State as special representative for the Presidential Rule of Law Initiative, he conceived and led the U.S.-China legal cooperation initiative agreed to by Presidents Bill Clinton and Jiang Zemin at their 1997–98 summit meetings. He accompanied President Clinton to China in 1998. Before joining the Yale Law School faculty, Professor Gewirtz served as law clerk to Justice Thurgood

Marshall of the U.S. Supreme Court and practiced law at the Washington, DC, law firm of Wilmer, Cutler & Pickering.

Maurice R. Greenberg* is chairman and CEO of C.V. Starr & Co., Inc. Mr. Greenberg retired as chairman and CEO of American International Group, Inc. (AIG) in March 2005. Mr. Greenberg is former chairman of the Asia Society. He is the founding chairman of the U.S.-Philippine Business Committee and vice chairman of the U.S.-ASEAN Business Council. He is a member of the U.S.-China Business Council. He served on the President's Advisory Committee for Trade Policy and Negotiations and the Business Roundtable. He is the past chairman, deputy chairman, and director of the Federal Reserve Bank of New York.

Harry Harding* is university professor of international affairs at the George Washington University, and a visiting fellow in the Center on U.S.-China Relations at the Asia Society. From 2005–2007, he was director of research and analysis at Eurasia Group, a political risk research and consulting firm headquartered in New York. He remains a counselor to Eurasia Group and chair of its China Task Force. Dr. Harding has served on the faculties of Swarthmore College (1970–71) and Stanford University (1971–83), was a senior fellow in the Foreign Policy Studies Program at the Brookings Institution (1983–94), and was dean of the Elliott School of International Affairs at the George Washington University (1995–2005).

Carla A. Hills is chairman and CEO of Hills & Company, International Consultants, which advises companies on global trade and investment issues. Ambassador Hills served as U.S. trade representative in the first Bush administration, and as secretary of the U.S. Department of Housing and Urban Development and assistant attorney general, Civil Division, U.S. Department of Justice, in the Ford administration.

Frank Sampson Jannuzi is Hitachi International Affairs fellow of the Council on Foreign Relations, currently serving as a visiting scholar at Keio University and a visiting researcher at the Institute of International

Policy Studies in Tokyo. Jannuzi served as the East Asia adviser to the Democratic staff of the Senate Foreign Relations Committee (1997–2006) and as the East Asia political-military analyst in the Bureau of Intelligence and Research, U.S. Department of State (1989–97).

Michael H. Jordan is chairman of the board and CEO of EDS Corporation. He joined EDS in March 2003. Jordan is the retired chairman and CEO of CBS Corporation (formerly Westinghouse Electric Corporation). Mr. Jordan is a member of the following organizations: the National Foreign Trade Council, the Brookings Institution, the U.S.-Japan Business Council, the Council on Foreign Relations, the United Negro College Fund, the Business Council, the United States Council for International Business, the Business Roundtable, and the International Advisory Board of British-American Business Inc. He is also a director of Viventure Partners; and a director of Aetna, Inc.

Virginia Ann Kamsky* is the founder, CEO, and chairman of the board of Kamsky Associates, Inc. (KAI), established in 1980 and the first foreign investment firm approved to operate in China. Ms. Kamsky is the chairman of the board of trustees of the China Institute in America and a director of the National Committee on U.S.-China Relations. Prior to founding KAI, Ms. Kamsky was an officer of Chase Bank and served as a member of the first official U.S. banking delegation to China in 1978, when normalization of diplomatic relations between the United States and China was announced. She has served on several corporate boards, including W.R. Grace and currently, the board of directors of Olin Corporation.

David M. Lampton is dean of faculty and director of China studies at Johns Hopkins-SAIS and director of Chinese studies at the Nixon Center in Washington, DC. Formerly he was president of the National Committee on U.S.-China Relations in New York City (1988–97). He is the author of *Same Bed, Different Dreams: Managing U.S.-China Relations, 1989–2000* and editor of *The Making of Chinese Foreign and Security Policy in the Era of Reform*. He is currently working on a book on China's power and what it means for the world.

Nicholas R. Lardy is a senior fellow at the Peterson Institute for International Economics in Washington, DC. Previously he was a senior fellow at the Brookings Institution (1995–2003) and the director of the Henry M. Jackson School of International Studies at the University of Washington (1991–95). Dr. Lardy serves on the board of directors and executive committee of the National Committee on U.S.-China Relations; is a member of the Council on Foreign Relations; and is a member of the editorial board of the *China Quarterly,* the *China Review,* and the *China Economic Review.*

Herbert Levin* focused on China and Asia in his work in Washington on the staffs of the Policy Planning Council, National Intelligence Council, and National Security Council, and during his thirty-four years as a Foreign Service officer. Thereafter he was for five years in the office of UN Undersecretary-General Ji Chaozhu. For the next five years he served as executive director of the America-China Society for cochairmen Cyrus Vance and Henry Kissinger. Mr. Levin has degrees from Harvard and the Fletcher School of Law and Diplomacy. He served in the U.S. Army, Far East Command, Tokyo.

Cheng Li is William R. Kenan professor of government at Hamilton College, New York. He is currently a visiting fellow at the John L. Thornton China Center in the foreign policy studies program of the Brookings Institution, a director of the National Committee on U.S.-China Relations, and a trustee of the Institute of Current World Affairs. His publications include *Rediscovering China: Dynamics and Dilemmas of Reform* (1997), *China's Leaders: The New Generation* (2001), and the edited volume *Bridging Minds Across the Pacific: The Sino-U.S. Educational Exchange, 1978–2003* (2005). Dr. Li is currently working on two book manuscripts: *Chinese Technocrats* and *Urban Subcultures in Shanghai.*

Winston Lord* is currently cochair of the Overseers of the International Rescue Committee. His government service has included assistant secretary of state for East Asian and Pacific affairs for President Clinton; ambassador to China for President Reagan; director of the State Department's policy planning staff; and special assistant to the National Security

Adviser for Presidents Ford and Nixon. Lord's service outside the government has included president of the Council on Foreign Relations and chairman of the National Endowment for Democracy.

Xiaobo Lu is director of the Weatherhead East Asian Institute and professor of political science at Barnard College and Columbia University. He is the author of the book *Cadres and Corruption* (2000). His recent book (with Thomas Bernstein) is on the political and economic changes in the Chinese countryside, *Taxation Without Representation in Contemporary Rural China* (2003). From 2003–2004, he was a visiting professor at Tsinghua University in Beijing, Jiaotong University in Shanghai, and senior research fellow at City University of Hong Kong.

Evan S. Medeiros is currently a political scientist at the RAND Corporation in Washington, DC. His research interests include China's foreign and national security policies, U.S.-China relations, and Chinese defense industrial issues. Prior to joining RAND, Dr. Medeiros was a senior research associate for East Asia at the Monterey Institute's Center for Nonproliferation Studies in Monterey, CA. In 2000, he was a visiting fellow at the Institute of American Studies at the China Academy of Social Sciences (CASS) in Beijing and an adjunct lecturer at China's Foreign Affairs College. He recently completed a book manuscript for Stanford University Press on the evolution of Chinese policies on weapons nonproliferation. He travels to Asia frequently.

James C. Mulvenon is deputy director, advanced analysis at Defense Group Inc.'s Center for Intelligence Research and Analysis. A specialist on the Chinese military, Dr. Mulvenon's research focuses on Chinese C4ISR (command, control, communications, computers, intelligence, and reconnaissance); defense research, development, acquisition organizations and policy; strategic weapons programs (computer network attack and nuclear warfare); cryptography; and the military and civilian implications of the information revolution in China.

Andrew J. Nathan is Class of 1919 professor and chair of the department of political science at Columbia University. His publications include *Chinese Democracy* (1985); *The Great Wall and the Empty Fortress: China's Search for Security,* with Robert S. Ross (1997); *The Tiananmen Papers,* edited with Perry Link (2001); and *China's New Rulers: The Secret Files,* with Bruce Gilley (2002, second edition 2003). He serves on the boards of Human Rights in China and Freedom House and on the Asia Advisory Committee of Human Rights Watch.

Stephen A. Orlins is president of the National Committee on U.S.-China Relations. Prior to becoming president, Mr. Orlins was the managing director of Carlyle Asia, one of Asia's largest private equity funds. From 1983 to 1991, Mr. Orlins was with the investment banking firm of Lehman Brothers where he was a managing director from 1985 to 1991 and president of Lehman Brothers Asia from 1987 to 1990. Mr. Orlins also has practiced law with Coudert Brothers and Paul, Weiss, Rifkind, Wharton & Garrison in New York, Hong Kong, and Beijing. From 1976 to 1979, Mr. Orlins served in the office of the legal adviser of the U.S. Department of State, where he was a member of the legal team that helped establish diplomatic relations with the People's Republic of China.

Evans J.R. Revere assumed the presidency of the Korea Society in New York City in January 2007. Prior to becoming president, Mr. Revere was a career U.S. diplomat and one of the U.S. Department of State's leading Asia experts. His last State Department assignment was as Cyrus Vance fellow in diplomatic studies at the Council on Foreign Relations, where he helped launch its Independent Task Force on U.S.-China relations and served as the Task Force's first project director. Mr. Revere previously served as acting assistant secretary of state for East Asian and Pacific affairs and principal deputy assistant secretary in that bureau, managing U.S. relations with the Asia-Pacific region and leading an organization of 950 American diplomats and some 2,500 Foreign Service national employees. His diplomatic career included service in the PRC, Taiwan, the Republic of Korea, and Japan, and extensive experience in negotiations with North Korea.

Bradley H. Roberts is a member of the research staff at the Institute for Defense Analyses (IDA) in Alexandria, Virginia. He also serves as an adjunct professor at George Washington University and as a member of the board of directors of the U.S. committee of the Council for Security Cooperation in the Asia Pacific (CSCAP). Prior to joining IDA in 1995, Dr. Roberts was editor of the *Washington Quarterly* and a member of the research staff at the Center for Strategic and International Studies. He is also coauthor with Robert A. Manning and Ronald Montaperto of *China, Nuclear Weapons, and Arms Control* (2000).

Alan D. Romberg is director of the East Asia program at the Henry L. Stimson Center. Immediately prior to that, Mr. Romberg was principal deputy director of the U.S. Department of State policy planning staff (1994–98), senior adviser and director of the Washington office of the U.S. permanent representative to the United Nations (1998–99), and special assistant to the secretary of the Navy (1999–2000). He was director of research and studies at the United States Institute of Peace in 1994, following almost ten years as C.V. Starr senior fellow for Asian studies at the Council on Foreign Relations (1985–94). A Foreign Service officer for over twenty years, he was principal deputy assistant secretary of state and deputy spokesman of the department (1981–85). His latest book is *Rein In at the Brink of the Precipice: American Policy Toward Taiwan and U.S.-PRC Relations* (2003).

Randy Schriver* is one of five founding partners of Armitage International L.C. Immediately prior to his return to the private sector, he served as deputy assistant secretary of state for East Asian and Pacific affairs responsible for the PRC, Taiwan, Mongolia, Hong Kong, Australia, New Zealand, and the Pacific Islands. He has also served in the office of the secretary of defense, and was an active-duty navy intelligence officer who served in the first Gulf War.

Wendy R. Sherman is a founding principal of the Albright Group, LLC, a global advisory firm and Albright Capital Management, LLC, an investment advisory firm focused on emerging markets. She has served as counselor of the Department of State, special adviser to the president and secretary of state on North Korea, and assistant secretary of state for legislative affairs, which included responsibility for securing the department's more than $23 billion annual budget appropriation. As a chief troubleshooter to two secretaries of state, Ambassador Sherman's portfolio included Asia, the Middle East, Central America, North Korea, Russia, and Cuba, as well as transnational issues.

Arthur Waldron* is the Lauder professor of international relations at the University of Pennsylvania. He received his BA from Harvard (summa cum laude, valedictorian) in 1971 and his PhD, also from Harvard, in 1981. He lived in Asia for four years, studying Chinese and Japanese. Earlier in his career he spent a year in England, a semester in France, and a semester at (then) Leningrad State University. He has also taught as visiting professor at the Catholic University of Leuven in Belgium and been a visiting fellow at the Institute of Southeast Asian Studies in Singapore. He has written three books in English and edited four more, including two in Chinese. His works have been translated into Chinese, Italian, Korean and Japanese. Professor Waldron is a member of the board of directors of Freedom House and of the Jamestown Foundation, and vice president of the International Assessment and Strategy Center, a nonpartisan, nonprofit research organization based in Alexandria, Virginia. He has been a regular visitor to China for nearly thirty years.

Task Force Observers

Jerome A. Cohen
Council on Foreign Relations

Elizabeth C. Economy
Council on Foreign Relations

Adam Segal
Council on Foreign Relations

Recent Independent Task Force Reports
Sponsored by the Council on Foreign Relations

National Security Consequences of U.S. Oil Dependency (2006); John Deutch and James R. Schlesinger, Chairs; David G. Victor, Project Director

Russia's Wrong Direction: What the United States Can and Should Do (2006); John Edwards and Jack Kemp, Chairs; Stephen Sestanovich, Project Director

More than Humanitarianism: A Strategic U.S. Approach Toward Africa (2006); Anthony Lake and Christine Todd Whitman, Chairs; Princeton N. Lyman and J. Stephen Morrison, Project Directors

In the Wake of War: Improving U.S. Post-Conflict Capabilities (2005); Samuel R. Berger and Brent Scowcroft, Chairs; William L. Nash, Project Director; Mona K. Sutphen, Deputy Director

In Support of Arab Democracy: Why and How (2005); Madeleine K. Albright and Vin Weber, Chairs; Steven A. Cook, Project Director

Building a North American Community (2005); John P. Manley, Pedro Aspe, and William F. Weld, Chairs; Thomas P. d'Aquino, Andrés Rozental, and Robert A. Pastor, Vice Chairs; Chappel A. Lawson, Project Director; Cosponsored with the Canadian Council of Chief Executives and the Consejo Mexicano de Asuntos Internacionales

Iran: Time for a New Approach (2004); Zbigniew Brzezinski and Robert M. Gates, Chairs; Suzanne Maloney, Project Director

Renewing the Atlantic Partnership (2004); Henry A. Kissinger and Lawrence H. Summers, Chairs; Charles A. Kupchan, Project Director

Nonlethal Weapons and Capabilities (2004); Graham T. Allison and Paul X. Kelley, Chairs; Richard L. Garwin, Project Director

New Priorities in South Asia: U.S. Policy Toward India, Pakistan, and Afghanistan (2003); Frank G. Wisner II, Nicholas Platt, and Marshall M. Bouton, Chairs; Dennis Kux and Mahnaz Ispahani, Project Directors; Cosponsored with the Asia Society

Finding America's Voice: A Strategy for Reinvigorating U.S. Public Diplomacy (2003); Peter G. Peterson, Chair; Jennifer Sieg, Project Director

Emergency Responders: Drastically Underfunded, Dangerously Unprepared (2003); Warren B. Rudman, Chair; Richard A. Clarke, Senior Adviser; Jamie F. Metzl, Project Director

Chinese Military Power (2003); Harold Brown, Chair; Joseph W. Prueher, Vice Chair; Adam Segal, Project Director

Iraq: The Day After (2003); Thomas R. Pickering and James R. Schlesinger, Chairs; Eric P. Schwartz, Project Director

Threats to Democracy (2002); Madeleine K. Albright and Bronislaw Geremek, Chairs; Morton H. Halperin, Project Director; Elizabeth Frawley Bagley, Associate Director

America—Still Unprepared, Still in Danger (2002); Gary Hart and Warren B. Rudman, Chairs; Stephen Flynn, Project Director

Terrorist Financing (2002); Maurice R. Greenberg, Chair; William F. Wechsler and Lee S. Wolosky, Project Directors

Enhancing U.S. Leadership at the United Nations (2002); David Dreier and Lee H. Hamilton, Chairs; Lee Feinstein and Adrian Karatnycky, Project Directors

Testing North Korea: The Next Stage in U.S. and ROK Policy (2001); Morton I. Abramowitz and James T. Laney, Chairs; Robert A. Manning, Project Director

The United States and Southeast Asia: A Policy for the New Administration (2001); J. Robert Kerrey, Chair; Robert A. Manning, Project Director

Strategic Energy Policy: Challenges for the 21st Century (2001); Edward L. Morse, Chair; Amy Myers Jaffe, Project Director

---

All publications listed are available on the Council on Foreign Relations website, CFR.org.
To order printed copies, contact the Brookings Institution Press: 800-537-5487.